The **OFFICIAL DVSA GUIDE** to
LEARNING
TO DRIVE

London: TSO

Written and compiled by the Learning Materials section of the Driver and Vehicle Standards Agency.

© Crown Copyright 2017

Previously known as *Your Driving Test* (First edition 1990) and *The Official Driving Test* (Third edition 1996)

Current title: *The Official DVSA Guide to Learning to Drive*

Tenth edition 2017
Third impression 2018

ISBN 978 0 11 5535505
A CIP catalogue record for this book is available from the British Library.

Other titles in the Driving Skills series

The Official DVSA Guide to Driving – the essential skills
The Official DVSA Guide to Better Driving
The Official DVSA Theory Test for Car Drivers
The Official DVSA Theory Test for Car Drivers (DVD-ROM)
The Official DVSA Guide to Hazard Perception (DVD-ROM)

The Official DVSA Theory Test Kit iPhone/Android App
The Official DVSA Highway Code iPhone App
The Official DVSA Hazard Perception Practice iOS App

The Official DVSA Guide to Riding – the essential skills
The Official DVSA Theory Test for Motorcyclists
The Official DVSA Theory Test for Motorcyclists (DVD-ROM)
The Official DVSA Guide to Learning to Ride
Better Biking – the official DVSA training aid (DVD)

The Official DVSA Guide to Driving Buses and Coaches
The Official DVSA Guide to Driving Goods Vehicles
The Official DVSA Theory Test for Drivers of Large Vehicles
The Official DVSA Theory Test for Drivers of Large Vehicles (DVD-ROM)
Driver CPC – the official DVSA guide for professional bus and coach drivers
Driver CPC – the official DVSA guide for professional goods vehicle drivers

The Official DVSA Guide to Tractor and Specialist Vehicle Driving Tests (eBook)
The Official DVSA Theory Test for Approved Driving Instructors (DVD-ROM)

We're turning over a new leaf.

Find us online

▶ GOV.UK – Simpler, clearer, faster

GOV.UK is the best place to find government services and information for

- car drivers
- motorcyclists
- driving licences
- driving and riding tests
- towing a caravan or trailer
- medical rules
- driving and riding for a living
- online services.

Visit **www.gov.uk** and try it out.

You can also find contact details for DVSA and other motoring agencies like DVLA at **www.gov.uk**

You'll notice that links to **GOV.UK**, the UK's new central government site, don't always take you to a specific page. This is because this new kind of site constantly adapts to what people really search for and so such static links would quickly go out of date. Try it out. Simply search what you need from your preferred search site or from **www.gov.uk** and you should find what you're looking for. You can give feedback to the Government Digital Service from the website.

**Driver & Vehicle
Standards
Agency**

The Driver and Vehicle Standards Agency (DVSA) is an executive agency of the Department for Transport.

We improve road safety in Great Britain by setting standards for driving and motorcycling, and making sure drivers, vehicle operators and MOT garages understand and follow roadworthiness standards. We also provide a range of licensing, testing, education and enforcement services.

www.gov.uk/dvsa

The Driver and Vehicle Agency (DVA) is an executive agency within the Department of the Environment for Northern Ireland.

Its primary aim is to promote and improve road safety through the advancement of driving standards and implementation of the government's policies for improving the mechanical standards of vehicles.

nidirect.gov.uk/motoring

Contents

01 Getting started

A message from the Chief Driving Examiner	9
Before you start	10
Structured learning	12
Your instructor	14
Official study aids	16
Practising	18
Notes for the accompanying driver	19

02 Key skills

Using this book	21
Legal responsibilities	22
Cockpit checks	24
Safety checks	26
Controls and instruments	28
Moving away and stopping	30
Safe positioning	32
Mirrors – vision and use	34
Signals	36
Anticipation and planning	38
Use of speed	40
Other traffic	42
Junctions	44
Roundabouts	46
Dual carriageways	48
Pedestrian crossings	50
Turning the vehicle around	52
Reversing	54
Parking	56
Emergency stop	59
Independent driving	61

Darkness	63
Weather conditions	65
Environmental issues	67
Passengers and loads	69
Security	71
Learning to drive on the motorway	73

03 Accompanying driver advice

Accompanying a learner	75
Getting started	76
Attitude	81
Planning	83
Legal responsibilities	86
Cockpit checks	87
Safety checks	88
Controls and instruments	89
Moving away and stopping	90
Safe positioning	91
Mirrors – vision and use	92
Signals	93
Anticipation and planning	94
Use of speed	95
Other traffic	97
Junctions	99
Roundabouts	101
Dual carriageways	102
Pedestrian crossings	103
Turning the vehicle around	104
Reversing	105
Parking	106
Emergency stop	107
Independent driving	108
Darkness	109

Weather conditions 110
Environmental issues 111
Passengers and loads 112
Security 113

04 The test and beyond

Are you ready for your test? 115
Booking your practical driving test 117
The day of your test 119
The practical test 121
Your test result 126
Pass Plus 128
Developing your driving skills 129

05 Other tests

Towing a trailer 131
Retest for those who have lost their licence 140

Annex

Private practice record 142

section **one**
GETTING STARTED

This section covers
- Before you start
- Structured learning
- Your instructor
- Official study aids
- Practising
- Notes for the accompanying driver

A message from the Chief Driving Examiner

Being able to drive on your own opens up a whole new world of independence. But, before you apply to take your practical test, you must have the skills and mindset you'll need to drive independently.

In this book, we explain the skills you need to understand and master before taking your test. We refer to the *Driver's Record*; if you don't have one of these, ask your instructor for a copy, or you can download one from **www.gov.uk**

You need to be capable of driving consistently, without help or prompting, to Level 5 in the *Driver's Record* before you take your practical test. Most people fail their test because they're not fully prepared, so make sure that you've covered all the key skills to the standard we show in this book.

The best way to gain these skills is to take enough lessons with an approved driving instructor, and get plenty of practice. You should aim to gain experience driving in varying traffic conditions, on different types of road and under a wide range of differing weather conditions.

Once you have the relevant skills and experience, and you've developed the right attitude, you'll be ready for a lifetime of safe driving.

Mark Winn

Mark Winn
Chief Driving Examiner

Before you start

First things first

You've decided you want to learn to drive. This will give you the opportunity to learn a completely new skill, one that will open up a whole new world of independence. But driving also comes with responsibility – it's important that you know how to drive safely and responsibly, that you learn the skills and that you practise. The aim is that you become a safe driver – not just to pass the test, but for life.

The first step is getting a provisional driving licence, but even before that you have to know that your eyesight is good enough to drive on the road.

Your eyesight

You **MUST** be able to read (with glasses or contact lenses, if necessary) a car number plate made after 1 September 2001 from 20 metres. If glasses or corrective lenses are required to read the number plate, they must be used while driving/riding.

You must also meet the minimum eyesight standard for visual acuity and have an adequate field of vision. An optician can tell you about this and carry out tests if necessary. For more information on drivers' eyesight requirements, please see **www.gov.uk**

Number plates

Most cars on the road today have number plates like this one

ABOI DVL

area identifier | age identifier | random letters

If you've had sight correction surgery, you should declare this when you apply for your provisional licence.

You're responsible for ensuring that your eyesight meets the minimum legal requirements every time you drive. The police can stop you at any time and ask you to take an eyesight test. You'll also have to take one at the start of your practical test.

Applying for your licence

You must be at least 17 years old before you can get a provisional car licence. However, as an exception, you can drive a car when you're 16 if you get, or have applied for, the enhanced rate of the mobility component of Personal Independence Payment (PIP).

> **Remember,** you must have received your provisional driving licence before you start to drive on the road. This means that you must actually have it in your possession, not just have sent away for it.

Driving licences are issued by the Driver and Vehicle Licensing Agency (DVLA). You can get an application form (D1) from any post office or request one online at **www.gov.uk**

Please note that you can **only** book your theory or practical driving test by post if you're paying by cheque or postal order.

In Northern Ireland, the issuing authority is the Driver and Vehicle Agency (Licensing) (DVA) and the form is a DL1. For more information, see **nidirect.gov.uk/ information-and-services/motoring/ learners-and-new-drivers**

Send your completed form to the appropriate office (details are given on the form). Remember to include a passport-type photograph, as all provisional licences now issued are photocard licences.

When you receive your provisional licence, check that all the details are correct. If you need to contact DVLA or DVA, you can do so via **www.gov.uk** and **nidirect.gov.uk/ motoring**

Structured learning

Learners who pass their driving test have had, on average, 40 to 50 hours of professional training combined with 20 hours of private practice. This shows the importance of combining professional training and private practice while you're learning to drive.

To help you learn in a structured way, DVSA has produced a *Driver's Record*.

The Driver's Record

The *Driver's Record* is a way of helping you and your driving instructor keep a record of your progress while you're learning to drive. You may have received one with your provisional licence. A copy of the *Driver's Record* can be downloaded – see page 13 for details of how to do this.

Following a structured learning programme, such as that contained in the *Driver's Record*, is beneficial to both you as a learner and your instructor. You need to learn the skill and then practise to get the experience.

You also need to learn both the theory and practical driving at the same time. This should help you to understand and apply the theory to actual driving.

The record is a pocket-sized leaflet that you should take with you to all your driving lessons.

The *Driver's Record* contains a list of all the key skills that you need to achieve in order to pass your test and become a safe driver. It has space for your instructor to fill in as you progress through the various levels shown on the record.

What are the five levels?

The meaning of each level is

1 the skill is introduced

2 it can be carried out under full instruction

3 it can be carried out correctly when prompted

4 it seldom needs to be prompted

5 you can carry it out consistently without any prompting

Levels 1 to 4 should be initialled and dated by your instructor, and full details added when you reach **Level 5**. From this, you and your instructor will be able to see at a glance which topics you need to improve. Details of the 25 key skills can be found on pages 20–71 of this book. Section 3 gives corresponding advice for an accompanying driver.

An important part of the structured learning process is practising what you've learnt during your lessons. Get together with your instructor and the person who will be helping you to practise, and discuss which areas you need to cover.

You can keep a record of any practice you have on different types of road and during different conditions between lessons on pages 142–143. Fill these in when you go out with the person helping you to practise. You can also record any worries you may have about your driving and then discuss these with your instructor. (Alternatively, printed sheets are available from your instructor.)

You aren't ready to take your test until you have a complete set of signatures in the **Level 5** boxes. Only then can your instructor sign the declaration.

> ### Where can I get hold of a Driver's Record?
>
> If you haven't got one, ask your instructor or download one by visiting **www.gov.uk**

By this time you should be able to drive safely without prompting.

Keep this as a record of your 'Learning to Drive' experience.

*The **Driver's Record**
will help to remind you what
you're trying to achieve,
how to get there and how
far you've got.*

Your instructor

If you're going to pay someone to teach you to drive, they must be an approved driving instructor (ADI) or hold a trainee licence.

DVSA is responsible for checking the instructional standards of ADIs. All ADIs must

- have held a full driving licence for at least four years
- pass a challenging theory and practical test
- reach and keep up a high standard of instruction. ADIs are regularly checked by DVSA
- be registered with DVSA
- display a green ADI identification certificate on the windscreen of the tuition vehicle during lessons.

It's unlikely that anyone except an ADI would have the experience, knowledge and training to teach you properly.

Some trainee driving instructors are granted a trainee licence so that they can gain teaching experience before their qualifying examination. This licence is a pink identification certificate and must be displayed on the windscreen of the tuition vehicle during lessons.

Choosing an ADI

Ask friends or relatives for recommendations. Choose an instructor who has a good reputation, is reliable and punctual, and whose car suits you. Ask the instructor for their grade before starting a course of lessons.

What does each instructor grade mean?

The standard of instruction of all ADIs is checked regularly by DVSA. The instructor is then given a grade.

A a high overall standard of instruction

B sufficient competence

Remember, you can always ask your instructor their grade.

Choosing the right instructor is vital to helping you develop as a driver. A good instructor will be happy to answer all your questions.

Ask if they've signed up to the industry code of practice. This is a voluntary code that covers the following

- their level of qualification
- the personal conduct expected from them when giving tuition
- the professional conduct of their business
- the acceptability of their advertising
- their method of dealing with complaints.

For further information or advice, visit **www.gov.uk** or telephone DVSA on **0300 200 1122**.

Take advice from your ADI Your instructor will be able to help with all aspects of driving and advise you on

- what to study – DVSA produces a range of books, eBooks, DVD-ROMs and apps to help you learn to drive
- how to practise and what you should be practising
- when you're ready for your test
- further training after you've passed your test (Pass Plus scheme – see page 128).

What if I find I don't like my instructor after I start lessons?

You can always find yourself a new instructor. It's important that you get on well with whoever is teaching you to drive. Different people prefer different teaching styles. You should try to find someone that suits you.

Can I have lessons in my own car?

Some instructors are prepared to give lessons in your own car, if you're lucky enough to have one. Ask about this when you first contact them, as some instructors won't do so for health and safety reasons.

Official study aids

Lessons and practice are the most important elements of learning to drive, but there's something you can do when you're not in the car. There are various books and electronic products to help you with all stages of driving – theory, hazard perception and practical.

The Official Highway Code Essential reading for all road users. This updated edition contains the very latest rules of the road and up-to-date legislation, and provides advice on road safety and best practice. (Now available as an eBook and an iPhone app.)

DVSA also produces a series of books and electronic products to provide you with a sound knowledge of driving skills.

The Official DVSA Theory Test for Car Drivers Includes revision questions and answers for the multiple choice part of the theory test and explains why the answers are correct. The revision questions are updated from time to time to reflect any changes in the actual test, so make sure that you have the latest version. If you're well prepared you won't find the questions difficult. This information is also produced in DVD-ROM format for those who prefer an interactive way of learning. In this format, you can take as many mock tests as you like before you take your real test.

You can buy official DVSA learning materials online at **safedrivingforlife.info/shop** or by calling our expert publications team on **0333 200 2401**. The team can give you advice about learning materials and how to prepare for the tests and beyond. They can also help you select a suitable learning material if you have a special need; for example, if you have a learning disability or English isn't your first language.

DVSA publications are also available from bookshops and online retailers. DVSA apps can be downloaded from the iOS App Store and eBooks are available from your device's eBook store.

The Official DVSA Guide to Hazard Perception (DVD-ROM) DVSA strongly recommends that you use this, preferably with your instructor, to prepare for the hazard perception part of the test. It's packed with useful tips, quizzes and expert advice. It also includes more than 100 interactive hazard perception clips, and your performance will receive a score so you'll know if you're ready to pass.

The Official DVSA Theory Test for Car Drivers and *The Official DVSA Guide to Hazard Perception* are available individually or packaged together as *The Official DVSA Complete Theory Test Kit,* which provides all the learning materials for the theory test in one package.

The Official DVSA Theory Test Kit App
The ideal way to prepare for your test on the go. The Theory Test Kit covers both the multiple choice and hazard perception parts of the test. Available from the iOS App Store and Google Play.

The Official DVSA Theory Test for Car Drivers Online This website provides you with instant access to all the latest DVSA theory test revision questions and answers.

You can start revising straight away on whatever smartphone, tablet, laptop or computer you have.

It's also packed with loads of helpful features so you get the most from your theory test revision. Simply choose the length of time that's right for you. Go to **dvsalearningzone.co.uk/shop/car-theory**

The Official DVSA Guide to Driving – the essential skills This book is referenced in section 2 (key skills). It contains a wealth of information about driving skills, from the basic, helping you when you first start to drive, through to in-depth advice about dealing with various road and traffic conditions.

Practising

The more driving experience you get, the better. You need to gain experience on all types of road and in different driving conditions. The more you practise and increase your experience, the more confident you'll become.

Your accompanying driver

The person helping you to practise must be at least 21 years old and have held a full EC/EEA licence for that type of car (automatic or manual) for at least the last three years. (Your accompanying driver can't ask for payment for helping you practise.)

The practice vehicle

The vehicle in which you practise must be roadworthy and properly insured for you to drive. If you drive while uninsured, you'll be committing a serious offence. The vehicle must also display L plates (or D plates in Wales) to the front and rear – make sure they're secure and don't obstruct your view.

Get together with both your instructor and the person who will be helping you to practise, so you can discuss what you need to do. Ask your instructor for advice on what skills you should practise after each lesson.

How to practise

You should vary what you do. Try to practise

- on as many types of road as you can

- in all sorts of traffic and weather conditions, even in the dark
- on dual carriageways where the national speed limit applies. You may be asked to drive on this type of road during your test.

When you practise, try to

- avoid obstructing other traffic. Most drivers are tolerant of learners, but don't try their patience too much
- consider the local residents. For example, don't repeatedly practise emergency stops in the same quiet residential streets or practise on test routes
- do lots of general driving. Don't just concentrate on the exercises included in the practical test.

Practising on motorways

Learner drivers can have driving lessons on motorways but only with an approved driving instructor (ADI) and in a car fitted with dual controls that's clearly displaying L plates.

Your ADI will be able to tell you when you're ready to take lessons on the motorway. This should be after you've had experience on a wide range of roads, and when you're just about ready to take your driving test. At this point, you should be a competent driver with an understanding of the theory of motorway driving.

Notes for the accompanying driver

Agreeing to accompany a learner is a responsibility not to be taken lightly. You'll be the person helping your learner get that important extra practice.

You must make sure that you have the right licence and that your car is insured for them to drive (see previous page). You'll also need L plates (D plates in Wales) and an additional interior mirror so that you can check what's happening behind.

When you accompany a learner, you're responsible for their actions. You'll need to stay calm and offer advice when needed. Have a chat with your learner and their instructor so that together you can decide what needs to be practised. Remember also that you **MUST NOT** use a mobile phone or other hand-held device while the provisional licence-holder is driving a motor vehicle on a road.

As the full licence-holder, you're still responsible for the vehicle while supervising the learner. You **cannot** concentrate fully, watch out for danger, or guide their actions safely while you're distracted by a phone conversation. You're breaking the law if you use your mobile while your learner is driving. **Don't take the chance.**

Everyone learns at a different pace and finds different things difficult. Something that you find easy may be difficult for a learner. Be patient and constructive. Make sure that you're aware of the standard that's expected of a learner driver and the style of driving they're being taught. Some things may have changed since you learnt to drive and it can be confusing for the learner to receive different messages.

Section 3 of this book contains lots of further advice aimed at the accompanying driver, covering all of the 25 key skills in addition to general hints and tips. Record your time spent in different situations on pages 142–143. This gives a permanent record of time spent and miles travelled and will help the three of you to work out where extra practice would be useful.

Learner drivers can have driving lessons on motorways. However, only a qualified approved driving instructor (ADI) can accompany a learner driver on a motorway driving lesson. See page 18.

> **Remember,** you can't receive payment for the time you spend helping your learner to practise.

section **two**
KEY SKILLS

This section covers

- Using this book
- Legal responsibilities
- Cockpit checks
- Safety checks

- Controls and instruments
- Moving away and stopping
- Safe positioning
- Mirrors – vision and use
- Signals
- Anticipation and planning
- Use of speed
- Other traffic
- Junctions
- Roundabouts
- Dual carriageways
- Pedestrian crossings
- Turning the vehicle around
- Reversing
- Parking
- Emergency stop
- Independent driving
- Darkness
- Weather conditions
- Environmental issues
- Passengers and loads
- Security

Using this book

Use this book as a reference while you're learning to drive. It can also be used to keep a record of your progress.

Reaching Level 5

All the key skills from the *Driver's Record* are shown on the following pages. On these pages, you'll find details of the standard you need to reach to become a safe driver in that skill and achieve a **Level 5** marking in your *Driver's Record*.

As your instructor signs off the skill in your *Driver's Record*, make a note on the relevant page in this book.

Expert tips

As well as explaining the level that you need to achieve, this section includes useful tips from the people who set the tests. These have been drawn up from years of experience and from common mistakes made by candidates during their driving tests.

Recap questions

For each skill there are recap questions – try answering these to refresh your memory.

All the answers to the recap questions can be found in the books referred to at the foot of the relevant pages.

What to expect on test

Once you've reached **Level 5** in all the key skills and are ready to take your test, there's some useful information about what to expect on the test and what the examiner will be looking for.

How do I use the references?

Further information about each of the skills can be found by following the references at the foot of the relevant pages. The reference **HC** refers to *The Official Highway Code* and the reference **DES** refers to *The Official DVSA Guide to Driving – the essential skills*.

The **HC** references are prefixed with either the letter **r** or **p**. The letter **r** indicates the rule number and the letter **p** indicates the page number.

The **DES** references are prefixed with the letter **s**. This indicates the section of the book.

See the example below.

References   **HC** r245, p35   **DES** s2

Legal responsibilities

As a driver, it's your responsibility to know how the law relates to both yourself and your vehicle, so make sure that you're up to date with the rules and regulations.

You need to comply with the **rules and regulations:**

 You're in a fit condition to drive safely

To do this, you need to understand how the following affects you

- **health** – certain medical conditions must be reported to DVLA (see **www.gov.uk** for details)

- **eyesight** – can you read a number plate as shown on page 10? If you need glasses to read it clearly, then you must always wear them when you're driving

- **drink** – don't drink and drive. There's a legal limit but it's safer not to drink at all if you're going to drive

- **drugs** – never take drugs before driving; the effects can be more severe than those caused by alcohol. Even some over-the-counter drugs can make you drowsy

- **tiredness** – if you're tired, you're more likely to have a collision. On a long journey, have a break every two hours or so

- **mobile phones** – it's illegal to use a hand-held phone while driving. Even a hands-free phone can distract you from your driving.

 You and the car you're driving comply with the regulations

To do this, you must ensure that

- the vehicle is taxed and has an MOT certificate if it needs one (see **www.gov.uk** for details)

- the vehicle is insured for you to drive

- the vehicle is in a roadworthy condition

- your driving licence is in order.

L plates should be clearly displayed on the front and back of the vehicle you're driving (D plates can be used in Wales).

Remember, you need to know the traffic rules and regulations – these can be found in The Highway Code. Make sure you know the regulations; ignorance is no defence.

What's the eyesight test?

You have to take an eyesight test before you start your practical test. Details of the requirements are given on page 10.

Who can teach me to drive?

Only ADIs and trainee licence-holders can teach for payment. They must display a badge on the windscreen during lessons.

Tips from the experts

Make sure that you know what to do if you're involved in a road traffic incident. Keep calm. As well as dealing with the scene of the incident, you may need to report it to the police.

Even hands-free phones distract you from your driving, so it's safer not to use one at all. Switch your phone off, otherwise you might be tempted to answer it if it rings. Stop safely to retrieve any messages.

The regulations about mobile phones also apply to the person accompanying you as you practise.

What to expect on test

You'll be asked about legal responsibilities during your theory test. You'll need to show the relevant papers and pass the eyesight test before starting your practical test.

Recap questions

Q1 *What are the legal requirements for someone helping a learner to drive?*

Q2 *What's the first thing you should do if you're involved in a road traffic incident?*

Accompanying driver advice   p84

Keep a record   Notes

Your instructor should keep a record of your progress on your *Driver's Record*. You may also like to fill in your progress below and make any notes that might help you in this space.

1	3	5
✓	✓	dd/mm/yy
introduced	prompted	independent

References   **HC** most of the code   **DES** s2

Cockpit checks

These checks may be simple, but they're essential. The car you're using needs to be comfortable and ready for you to drive before you turn the key in the ignition.

> You need to be able to do the following **consistently** and **without any help:**

Make sure the car is ready for you to drive

To do this, you need to check

- all doors are closed properly and the parking brake is on

- your seat is comfortable and in the correct position – if you have to adjust it, or your steering wheel, make sure they lock firmly in position

- the head restraint is properly adjusted – to give protection against whiplash injuries

- the mirrors are correctly adjusted – make sure that you check the interior and exterior mirrors so that you have the best view

- your seat belt is fastened, adjusted correctly and comfortable*

- the parking brake again and check that the gear lever is in neutral (if you're driving an automatic, that the gear lever is in P or N)

- whether you'll need to refuel your car.

Carry out the cockpit checks properly

To do this, you need to know

- the correct order in which to carry out the cockpit checks – you need to make sure that you're seated comfortably before you adjust your mirrors

- the best driving position

- how to adjust your mirrors, including adjusting them so that you're not dazzled by the driver behind you at night

- the various ways in which you can adjust your seat.

Remember, it's against the law not to have your seat belt fastened before you start to drive (unless you're exempt).* You're also responsible for making sure that any child under 14 who travels in your car wears a seat belt.

---

* If an inertia-reel seat belt has temporarily locked, because the vehicle is parked on a gradient, the driver may move the vehicle. As soon as the mechanism has released itself, the driver **MUST** stop and apply the belt.

Can I adjust the mirrors while I'm driving?

Never try to do this on the move – if you need to readjust your mirrors or seat position, find a safe place to stop first.

Do I need to do these checks every time?

Get into the habit of doing these checks every time – it's particularly important if other people use the car.

The rigid part of the restraint should support the back of your head.

Fasten your seat belt every time – it's against the law not to do so.

Make sure the gear lever is in neutral before starting the engine.

Tips from the experts

Make sure that you do these checks, in the right order, before you start the engine. This is particularly important if you're not the only person using the car.

What to expect on test

Your examiner will watch to make sure that you carry out all the checks, in the right order, before you start the engine.

Recap questions

Q1 *Is it the responsibility of the driver to make sure that adult passengers wear seat belts?*

Q2 *What could be a consequence of failing to carry out the cockpit checks properly?*

Q3 *Why should you check that the head restraint is in the correct position?*

Accompanying driver advice p85

Keep a record

Notes

Your instructor should keep a record of your progress on your *Driver's Record*. You may also like to fill in your progress below and make any notes that might help you in this space.

| 1 ✓ | 3 ✓ | 5 |
| introduced | prompted | dd/mm/yy |

| 2 ✓ | 4 ✓ | |
| full instruction | seldom prompted | independent |

References HC r97, 99   **DES** s3–5

Safety checks

It's important that your car is in good working order before you start the engine. You need to be aware of what to check, how to do it and how often to do it.

You need to be able to do the following **consistently** and **without any help:**

Carry out appropriate safety checks on your car

To do this, you need to check and know about

- **Petrol** – how to check the petrol level

- **Oil** – where and how to check the levels of engine oil and brake fluid

- **Water** – and other fluids, including screenwash and coolant – where they are and how to check them

- **Electrics** – front and rear lights, brake lights, hazard warning lights, indicators, horn and other warning devices – check they're clean and in good working order

- **Rubber** – the correct pressure for your tyres and how to measure it. Also, how to check tread depth and the tyre wall.

Also, you need to know how to check that the brakes and steering are working before you start to drive.

Understand the importance of good maintenance

To do this, you need to know about

- daily and weekly vehicle checks and how frequently each of the above checks should be made

- when your car requires professional maintenance, including the correct service intervals for your car

- what checks to make before starting a journey, especially longer ones

- how to clear and clean your windscreen so you get the best visibility at all times.

Remember, Petrol, Oil, Water, Electrics, Rubber. Just think POWER, then you shouldn't have any problems remembering your checks.

Can I check all this myself?

You'll need to get someone to help you check the brake lights. It's also easier and quicker to check the other lights if you can get someone to look while you're working the controls.

What kind of safety question will I be asked on test?

There are a limited number of safety-check questions that you can be asked on test. They will mostly take the form of 'show me' or 'tell me' questions and will relate to the subjects detailed on this page.

Tips from the experts

Make sure that you're familiar with the car you're driving, and that you can explain or demonstrate how you would carry out simple safety checks on that car.

You'll need to open the bonnet to carry out some of the checks – make sure that you know how to open the bonnet and also that you shut it properly once you've carried out the checks.

Regular servicing will keep the engine more efficient and save you money in the long run.

What to expect on test

The examiner will ask you

- one 'tell me' question at the beginning of your test, before you start driving. This is where you explain how you'd carry out a safety task
- one 'show me' question while you're driving; for example, showing how to wash the windscreen using the car controls.

Recap question

Q1 *What's the minimum tread depth for your car tyres?*

Accompanying driver advice | **p86**

Keep a record

Notes

Your instructor should keep a record of your progress on your *Driver's Record*. You may also like to fill in your progress below and make any notes that might help you in this space.

1 ✓	**3** ✓	**5**
introduced	prompted	dd/mm/yy
2 ✓	**4** ✓	
full instruction	seldom prompted	independent

References | **HC** r89, 97, p128 | **DES** s5, 14

Controls and instruments

You need to concentrate on what's happening around you when you're driving, so operating the vehicle's controls should be second nature.

You need to be able to do the following **consistently** and **without any help:**

 Operate the controls safely without looking

To do this, you need to be able to use the following controls correctly

- **foot controls** – the accelerator, clutch and footbrake pedals

- **hand controls** – the parking brake, steering wheel, indicators, headlights and gearstick

- **other controls** – the horn (you need to know when and for what reason you can legally use the horn), windscreen wipers, demister and heated windows. You also need to be aware of any controls specific to the car you're driving.

Remember, you need to be aware of the consequences of using the controls incorrectly.

 Read the various instruments of the car you're driving

To do this, you need to know

- the meaning and function of each element of the instrument panel, including the warning lights and speedometer.

Your speedometer
must show miles per hour and kilometres per hour.

Can I look at the gear lever?

If the car is moving, you shouldn't take your eyes off the road to look at the gear lever. You should already know which gear you're in. Don't coast with the gear lever in neutral or the clutch pedal down.

Should I steer and change gear at the same time?

For maximum control, you need both hands to steer. Try to change to the appropriate gear before starting to turn.

Tips from the experts

Make sure you're familiar with all the hand- and foot-operated controls before you start driving the car. You should be able to reach and operate all the controls while you're driving and without having to take your eyes off the road to find them.

On vehicles with manual transmission, there are three foot-operated controls: the accelerator, brake and clutch pedals. These controls should be used smoothly when moving off, accelerating, slowing and stopping. Harsh use of these controls will use more fuel than if they're used smoothly.

If you're driving a vehicle with automatic transmission, there will only be two foot-operated controls: the accelerator and the brake pedal.

To give yourself time to use the controls smoothly, look well ahead while you're driving. The earlier you see and start to respond to a hazard, the more time you'll have to respond smoothly and safely.

What to expect on test

Your examiner will want to see that you can

* demonstrate good control of the vehicle throughout the test
* show an understanding of the vehicle's instruments.

Recap question

Q1 *When is it illegal to use your horn?*

Accompanying driver advice	p87

Keep a record

Your instructor should keep a record of your progress on your *Driver's Record*. You may also like to fill in your progress below and make any notes that might help you in this space.

1 ✓	3 ✓	5
introduced	prompted	dd/mm/yy

2 ✓	4 ✓	
full instruction	seldom prompted	independent

Notes

References	**HC** r110	**DES** s3

Moving away and stopping

You have to move away and stop every time you drive and that's why it's so important to make sure that you know the correct way to move away and stop safely.

> You need to be able to do the following **consistently** and **without any help**:

LEVEL 5 — Move away and stop again safely

To do this, you need to

- be able to carry out both manoeuvres on level ground, on a hill, at an angle and straight ahead
- use the MSM and PSL routines
- observe what's happening around you and be aware of any blind spots
- coordinate your use of the accelerator, clutch and footbrake so that you move off and slow down safely and smoothly
- be able to use the parking brake and steering competently
- know where and when to look, what to look for and how to act safely on what you see
- be able to identify suitable stopping places
- know where and when to signal.

Remember, the MSM and PSL routines are key to virtually all aspects of driving.

Mirrors – Signal – Manoeuvre

M Use your **mirrors** to check the position of traffic around and behind you

S Show others what you intend to do. Always **signal** in good time

M A **manoeuvre** involves a change in position or speed.

Position – Speed – Look

P **Position** your car correctly for the move you want to make

S Adjust your **speed** so it's appropriate for the manoeuvre

L Have a final **look** to check it's safe before you start to steer.

What if I don't have a clear view of the road?

If you can't see because someone has parked close to you, edge out slowly and only move off when you can see it's safe.

How do I stop if someone is following very closely?

Make sure that you signal in good time to let them know that you're going to slow down and stop.

You may need to check your blind spot more than once when moving off from behind another car.

Tips from the experts

Always use your mirrors but only signal if you need to – don't just signal automatically.

Check your blind spots. Don't pull out without looking or make anyone else stop or swerve.

Move off smoothly in the correct gear and don't accelerate excessively.

What to expect on test

Your examiner may ask you to stop at the side of the road and then move away again. Every time you perform either of these manoeuvres, the examiner will watch your

- use of the controls and MSM routine each time you move off and stop – don't forget to incorporate the PSL routine when stopping

- observation of, and safe responses to, other road users

- judgement in selecting a safe and suitable place to stop.

Recap questions

Q1 *When would you not need to signal before moving away?*

Q2 *What are you looking for in a safe place to stop?*

Accompanying driver advice | p88

Keep a record

Notes

Your instructor should keep a record of your progress on your *Driver's Record*. You may also like to fill in your progress below and make any notes that might help you in this space.

1 ✓ introduced
2 ✓ full instruction
3 ✓ prompted
4 ✓ seldom prompted
5 dd/mm/yy independent

References | **HC** r103, 159–161, 238–252 | **DES** s5

Safe positioning

Make sure that you drive in the correct position for the road on which you're travelling. It's not only important for your safety but also for the safety of other road users.

You need to be able to do the following **consistently** and **without any help:**

 Keep a safe position during normal driving

To do this, you should be able to

- use the MSM and PSL routines (see page 30)
- follow the principles of lane discipline. Plan ahead and make sure that you move into the correct lane in good time
- show an understanding of how a wide or narrow road would affect the position you would choose
- keep a safe position during normal driving, especially around bends
- take up the correct position on a one-way street.

 Respond to the positions of other road users

To do this, you must understand

- how other vehicles, such as lorries and cyclists, need to position themselves
- what clearance you need to leave when passing stationary vehicles or obstructions.

Remember, plan ahead and make sure you move into the correct lane in good time. Don't change lanes at the last minute.

Always leave plenty of room *when passing a parked car, in case a door opens suddenly.*

How much room should I give a cyclist when overtaking?

Give them plenty of room – as much room as you would give a car. They may have to move away from the kerb in order to avoid something you can't see.

What if there are no markings on the road?

Position your vehicle sensibly even if there are no road markings. Don't drive too close to the kerb or too close to the centre of the road.

Tips from the experts

Don't obstruct other road users by being in the wrong lane, straddling lanes or swapping lanes unnecessarily.

At roundabouts, make sure that you don't cut across the path of other vehicles.

Make sure everyone around you knows where you want to go.

Follow the road markings and get into the correct lane as soon as possible.

What to expect on test

Your examiner will watch to make sure that you

- are using the MSM and PSL routines and acting on what you've seen
- respond to signs and road markings by selecting the correct lane in good time
- keep a safe position for the situation.

Recap questions

Q1 *When should you use the right-hand lane of a dual carriageway?*

Q2 *A large vehicle is emerging from a junction on the right. How might this affect your positioning?*

Q3 *Why is it important to move into the correct lane as soon as you can?*

Accompanying driver advice	p89

Keep a record

Notes

Your instructor should keep a record of your progress on your *Driver's Record*. You may also like to fill in your progress below and make any notes that might help you in this space.

1 ✓ introduced	3 ✓ prompted	5 dd/mm/yy
2 ✓ full instruction	**4** ✓ seldom prompted	independent

References	**HC** r127–146, 152–156	**DES** s7, 8

Mirrors – vision and use

Effective and well-timed observation should form part of your driving routine. You must know what's happening around you at all times and act safely on what you see.

You need to be able to do the following **consistently** and **without any help:**

 Effective use of all the mirrors at all times

To do this, you must know

- how to make use of the MSM and PSL routines (see page 30)

- when to use the mirrors and how often to use them

- why you need to use the mirrors and the importance of regular updates

- how to act on what you see in your mirrors.

 Show knowledge of how the mirrors differ

To do this, you need to know

- the uses for the interior mirror and the two exterior mirrors

- the effect that flat, concave and convex mirrors have, and how you interpret what you see in them

- what areas each mirror covers and where the blind spots are.

Remember, there are blind spots between what you can see when looking forward and what you can see in your mirrors. The car's bodywork also creates blind spots that can hide smaller road users. This picture highlights where these areas are.

How do I check my blind spots when I'm moving?

It's dangerous to look over your shoulder, as you may lose touch with what's happening in front, but you can give a quick sideways glance.

Which mirror should I look in first?

Normally you should look in the interior mirror first, followed by the exterior mirrors if necessary. Use of the exterior mirrors will depend on the situation.

Tips from the experts

Always look before you signal, look and signal before you act, and then act sensibly on what you see – just looking isn't enough to keep you safe.

Use all of your mirrors periodically while you drive, especially as you approach any hazard, so that you're constantly aware of what's happening around you.

Never manoeuvre before looking in your mirrors. Make sure that you always use your mirrors before

- moving off
- signalling
- turning left or right
- changing lanes or overtaking
- changing speed or stopping
- opening your car door.

What to expect on test

Your examiner will watch to make sure that you're aware of the scene all around, so you need to make sure that you use your mirrors and act safely on what you see.

Recap question

Q1 *What are the advantages and disadvantages of convex mirrors?*

Accompanying driver advice	p90

Keep a record

Notes

Your instructor should keep a record of your progress on your *Driver's Record*. You may also like to fill in your progress below and make any notes that might help you in this space.

1 ✓ introduced	**3** ✓ prompted	**5** dd/mm/yy
2 ✓ full instruction	**4** ✓ seldom prompted	independent

References	**HC** r161	**DES** s4

Signals

You need to understand, and respond safely to, signals given by other motorists and give clear, well-timed signals to other road users so that they know what you're planning to do.

> You need to be able to do the following **consistently** and **without any help:**

Give correct signals
To do this, you need to know

- why it's necessary to give signals – you need to signal to let others know what you intend to do

- when and how to give signals (it's important that you time your signal to allow others to respond safely)

- when and how to give arm signals

- when signals aren't required.

Read others' signals
To do this, you need to know

- the significance of other types of signal, including brake, reversing and hazard warning lights

- how to read signals given by traffic controllers such as the police.

School crossing patrols *may control traffic when schoolchildren are about. Always be ready for their signal to stop.*

 Remember, you should only use signals that are shown in The Highway Code.

Should I always signal?

There's no need to signal if there would be no benefit to other road users. If you have a clear view and can see that no-one else is around, there's no reason to signal.

Could I signal too early?

It could be confusing to signal too early – for example, if there are several side roads close together. Think about the situation before you give a signal.

1 Fog light

In seriously reduced visibility, fog lights can help to make vehicles easier to see

2 Reversing light

Shows a vehicle is about to reverse or is reversing. When you're reversing, it helps you to see what's behind you in the dark

3 Indicator light

Indicators normally show a change of direction. Both indicators flashing may mean a vehicle is stopped ahead

4 Rear/brake light

Brake lights can often be an early warning of what's happening further down the road

Tips from the experts

Don't be tempted to flash your headlights for any other reason than that shown in The Highway Code.

Always make sure to cancel your signal after you've carried out a manoeuvre. Leaving a signal on can lead to dangerous situations because other road users may take action based on the direction they expect you to go.

What to expect on test

The examiner will expect well-timed signals and safe responses to signals from others.

Recap questions

Q1 *When can you flash your headlights?*

Q2 *In what kind of situation would you not have to signal?*

Accompanying driver advice   **p91**

Keep a record   Notes

Your instructor should keep a record of your progress on your *Driver's Record*. You may also like to fill in your progress below and make any notes that might help you in this space.

1 introduced

3 prompted

5 dd/mm/yy

2 full instruction

4 seldom prompted

independent

References   **HC** r103–112, 116, p102   **DES** s5, 10

Anticipation and planning

These skills are found in all areas of driving. You should always be aware of what's going on around you while planning what you need to do in response.

> You need to be able to do the following **consistently** and **without any help:**

 Plan ahead and respond safely to others' actions

To do this, you need to be able to

- use the MSM and PSL routines (see page 30)
- identify hazards from clues and respond to them safely
- recognise times, places and conditions that mean there's a higher risk. This includes weather conditions
- use scanning techniques to enable you to plan ahead so that you can prioritise how you'll deal with hazards you encounter.

Remember, you'll need to plan ahead to deal with static hazards like traffic lights and roadworks.

 Anticipate the actions of all types of road user

To do this, you need to be familiar with the risks associated with each type of road user

- **cyclists** – take special care when you cross cycle lanes and watch out for cyclists passing on your left
- **motorcyclists** – look for them, especially at junctions and in slow-moving traffic
- **pedestrians** – take special care with the very young, older people and those with disabilities. They may not have seen you and could step out suddenly
- **animals** – give horse riders as much room as possible and pass them slowly
- **emergency vehicles** – don't panic, check where they're coming from and try to keep out of their way. If necessary, pull in to the side of the road and stop.

Can I use my hazard warning lights while I'm moving?

Yes, you can use them to warn other drivers of a hazard or an obstruction ahead, but only on a motorway or unrestricted dual carriageway. (On all other roads you must only use these lights when stationary.)

What do I gain from anticipating and planning?

If you scan ahead, you should be able to anticipate potentially hazardous situations. By being prepared, you minimise the element of surprise, leaving you to deal with situations safely and in a controlled way.

Tips from the experts

You need to be constantly checking what's going on in front, behind and around you. Planning ahead means that you won't find yourself in a situation where you have to stop suddenly.

Take every opportunity to look for clues such as reflections in windows or feet under a van, which might tell you what's going to happen next. Even when you're stationary the scene is constantly changing.

What to expect on test

You'll be expected to be aware of other road users and road and weather conditions at all times. You'll also need to show an awareness of the hazards they present and respond safely in good time.

Recap questions

Q1 *What hazards could you come across on a busy residential street?*

Q2 *Why might a motorcyclist need to swerve suddenly?*

If a cyclist looks over their shoulder, *hold back; they may be about to cross your path.*

Accompanying driver advice   **p92**

| **Keep a record** | Notes |

Your instructor should keep a record of your progress on your *Driver's Record*. You may also like to fill in your progress below and make any notes that might help you in this space.

1 ✓ introduced
2 ✓ full instruction
3 ✓ prompted
4 ✓ seldom prompted
5 dd/mm/yy independent

References   **HC** r146, 160–161, 204–237   **DES** s7, 10

Use of speed

Your speed should be based on various factors, including the condition of the road, weather and traffic, and the presence of pedestrians. Always drive within the speed limit.

You need to be able to do the following **consistently** and **without any help**:

 Drive at an appropriate speed for the conditions

To do this, you need to know

- national speed limits and restrictions for different types of road and any restricted speed limits for the road you're on

- the appropriate speed for particular road, weather and traffic conditions

- the appropriate speed to use where there are pedestrians and in traffic-calmed areas

- the stopping distance for your vehicle in different conditions and how to calculate a safe separation distance between yourself and the vehicle in front.

Never break the speed limit *– speed cameras are there to make sure everyone is driving within the speed limits.*

Remember, speed limits don't mean that you have to travel at that speed. Use your judgement and drive according to the conditions.

Can I exceed the speed limit to overtake someone?

No, you must always stay within the speed limit. It's illegal to break it, even for a short period of time. Driving faster is dangerous, and remember, speed kills.

Can I drive too slowly?

You should drive confidently and at a reasonable speed. If you drive too slowly or hesitate unnecessarily, it can be very frustrating for other drivers and can lead to road traffic incidents.

Tips from the experts

Don't drive too fast for the road and traffic conditions and make sure that you can stop safely, well within the distance you can see to be clear. Leave extra distance for stopping on wet or slippery roads.

Don't change your speed unpredictably.

Don't approach junctions too fast, or too slowly. Avoid being over-cautious – for example, by stopping and waiting when it's safe to go.

What to expect on test

Your examiner will watch how you control your speed throughout your test. They'll want to see that you can

- make reasonable progress along the road and respond to changing conditions
- keep up with other traffic but comply with the speed limits
- show confidence, together with sound judgement.

Recap questions

Q1 *What's the national speed limit for cars on a dual carriageway?*

Q2 *What separation distance should you leave between you and the vehicle in front on a wet road?*

Accompanying driver advice   **p93**

Keep a record   Notes

Your instructor should keep a record of your progress on your *Driver's Record*. You may also like to fill in your progress below and make any notes that might help you in this space.

1 ✓ introduced

2 ✓ full instruction

3 ✓ prompted

4 ✓ seldom prompted

5 dd/mm/yy independent

References   **HC** r124–126, p42–43   **DES** s7, 10

Other traffic

In most cases when you're driving, there will be other traffic on the road. You need to be able to deal safely and confidently when meeting, crossing and overtaking other vehicles.

> You need to be able to do the following **consistently** and **without any help:**

 Safely negotiate situations involving other traffic

To do this, you need to be confident when dealing with these situations

- **meeting** – where there are parked cars or obstructions on your side of the road, you must be prepared to give way to oncoming traffic. On narrow roads you may need to use passing places

- **crossing** – you normally need to cross the path of other traffic if you're turning right into a side road or driveway. Make sure that you position your car correctly, as close to the centre of the road as is safe, and watch out for oncoming traffic, stopping if necessary. Don't cut the corner or take the turn too widely

- **overtaking** – overtake only if you can do so legally and safely. Check the speed and position of any vehicles behind (they might be planning to overtake you), in front, and coming towards you before you decide to overtake.

 Understand the rules for dealing with traffic

To do this, you need to be aware of

- the MSM and PSL routines (see page 30)

- why and when to give way – you shouldn't cause another road user to slow down or alter their course when they have priority

- the significance of passing places, warning signs, road markings and how to deal with obstructions

- the importance of planning and anticipation, and acting safely on what you see

- how to drive on all road types, including a one-way or two-way road, a three-lane two-way road, a major or minor road, a narrow road and a dual carriageway.

Remember, don't overtake as you approach a junction. A vehicle may pull out of the junction into your path.

If a driver is indicating, can I pull out before they turn?

Always wait until you're sure they're turning before you move out. They may have forgotten to cancel their signal.

Can I flash my lights to give someone the go-ahead?

No. The Highway Code states that you should only flash your lights as a warning, to let someone know you're there.

Tips from the experts

When passing parked cars, watch out for doors opening, pedestrians (especially children) stepping out from between the cars, and vehicles pulling out.

When overtaking cyclists or horse riders, slow right down and give them as much room as you would a car.

If you're going to pass an obstruction or overtake, start planning early so that you get a better view of the road ahead.

What to expect on test

Your examiner will watch to see how you

- apply the MSM and PSL routines
- respond to road and traffic conditions
- handle the car's controls.

If there's an obstruction on your side of the road, plan ahead so that you can give way to oncoming traffic.

Recap questions

Q1 *Give three examples of where it's against the law to overtake*

Q2 *On which side can you pass traffic when on a one-way road?*

Q3 *You see a car coming towards you on a narrow road. There's a passing place just ahead on the other side of the road. What should you do?*

Accompanying driver advice | **p95**

Keep a record

Notes

Your instructor should keep a record of your progress on your *Driver's Record*. You may also like to fill in your progress below and make any notes that might help you in this space.

| **1** ✓ introduced | **3** ✓ prompted | **5** dd/mm/yy |
| **2** ✓ full instruction | **4** ✓ seldom prompted | independent |

References | **HC** r133–143, 146, 151–155, 162–168 **DES** s7, 8, 10

Junctions

There are many different types of junction. You need to be able to negotiate any junction on any type of road safely, without holding up other traffic unnecessarily.

You need to be able to do the following **consistently** and **without any help**:

 Safely negotiate all types of junction

To do this, you need to deal confidently with these junctions

- **T-junctions and Y-junctions** – you need to make sure that you position yourself so that you get the best view of the road into which you're turning

- **crossroads** – always check who has priority as you approach a crossroads and be aware of the movement of any other traffic

- **slip roads** – these are there to help you match your speed to that of the traffic on the main road

- **unmarked junctions** – be cautious as no-one has priority here

- **junctions on all types of road** – urban and rural roads, dual carriageways and one-way streets.

 Understand the rules for dealing with junctions

To do this, you need to be aware of the

- MSM and PSL routines (see page 30)

- rules for turning at, entering into and emerging from a junction. These include the need to position your car correctly, adjust your speed and stop if necessary

- significance of advance warning signs and road markings, and acting correctly on what you see

- rules of priority, especially when dealing with unmarked junctions

- importance of good observation.

Remember, you need to look both ways, even if you're turning left – there may be another vehicle on your side of the road.

What if a pedestrian is crossing the road into which I'm turning?

You should be checking as you approach the turning. A pedestrian who has already started to cross has priority, so give way. Remember, they might not have seen you.

How can I improve my view of the road into which I'm turning?

Sometimes buildings, hedges, bends in the road or parked cars can obscure your view. Edge forward slowly until you can see the road clearly before you pull out.

Tips from the experts

In a one-way street, move into the correct lane as soon as you can do so safely.

When approaching a junction, make sure that you slow down in good time so that you don't have to brake harshly if you need to stop.

Watch out for pedestrians, cyclists and motorcyclists when you're turning, as they're not as easy to see as larger vehicles.

Usually, when emerging from a junction, you should keep well to the left if you're turning left. If you're turning right, keep as close to the centre of the road as is safe.

What to expect on test

Your examiner will watch carefully to take account of your

- use of the MSM and PSL routines
- position and speed on approach to the junctions
- observation and judgement.

Recap questions

Q1 *When can you wait on the yellow crisscross lines at a box junction?*

Q2 *Who has priority if there are no road markings at a crossroads?*

Q3 *How should you negotiate a traffic-light-controlled junction that has an advanced stop line for cyclists?*

Accompanying driver advice   **p97**

Keep a record

Notes

Your instructor should keep a record of your progress on your *Driver's Record*. You may also like to fill in your progress below and make any notes that might help you in this space.

1 ✓ introduced

2 ✓ full instruction

3 ✓ prompted

4 ✓ seldom prompted

5 dd/mm/yy independent

References   **HC** r170–183   **DES** s8

Roundabouts

To deal with roundabouts safely and confidently, you should have a thorough understanding of the rules that apply when approaching and negotiating them.

You need to be able to do the following **consistently** and **without any help:**

 Safely negotiate different types of roundabout

To do this, you need to be confident at dealing with these junctions

- **standard roundabouts** – you should know how to approach and negotiate roundabouts even when there are no road markings directing you into particular lanes

- **mini-roundabouts** – you'll probably need to adjust your speed on approach because there's less room to manoeuvre and less time to signal

- **multiple and satellite roundabouts** – assess the layout of the roundabouts by looking at the signs on approach. Treat each roundabout separately and apply the normal rules

- **traffic-light-controlled roundabouts** – priorities will often be different from normal roundabouts here.

 Understand the rules for dealing with roundabouts

To do this, you need to be aware of

- how and when to apply the MSM and PSL routines (see page 30)

- the importance of effective observation and awareness of the traffic around you

- how to position your car correctly and which lane to use, both as you approach and when you're on a roundabout

- who has priority when you're entering a roundabout

- the procedure for leaving a roundabout.

Remember, look at all the road signs and markings, and make sure you get into the correct lane for the direction you want to take in good time.

What if there's a long vehicle at the roundabout?

Stay well back and give them plenty of room. They might need to take a different course as they approach and go around the roundabout.

When should I start indicating to show I'm taking an exit?

You need to turn your left indicator on just after you've passed the exit before the one that you want to take. Remember to cancel it once you've finished turning.

Tips from the experts

Approach the roundabout at the correct speed so that you can assess other traffic using the roundabout. If you need to stop, avoid braking harshly.

Roundabouts are there to help traffic move freely. Don't stop unless you need to.

If you're in a queue, don't move forward before checking that the vehicle in front of you is moving. They may be more hesitant than you.

What to expect on test

Your examiner will take account of your ability to deal with roundabouts without undue hesitation. This will include your use of the MSM and PSL routines, your position, speed on approach, observation and judgement throughout.

Recap question

Q1 *Why would a cyclist signal right but stay in the left-hand lane as they approach a roundabout?*

Accompanying driver advice	p99

Keep a record   Notes

Your instructor should keep a record of your progress on your *Driver's Record*. You may also like to fill in your progress below and make any notes that might help you in this space.

1 ✓ introduced
3 ✓ prompted
5 dd/mm/yy

2 ✓ full instruction
4 ✓ seldom prompted
5 independent

References	**HC** r184–190	**DES** s8

Dual carriageways

You join some dual carriageways from a slip road, in a similar way to joining a motorway. You should be confident using these high-speed roads where traffic can cross and turn right.

You need to be able to do the following **consistently** and **without any help**:

 Drive safely on all types of dual carriageway

To do this, you need to drive confidently when

- using urban and rural dual carriageways and clearways
- joining a dual carriageway – if there's a slip road, use it to adjust your speed to match any vehicles on the dual carriageway and join where there's a suitable gap. If there's no slip road, join as you would on any other road
- travelling on a dual carriageway – choose the correct lane. When leaving, you should move into the correct lane in good time
- turning right off a dual carriageway where allowed.

Remember, if you have to stop at the end of a slip road, it may be difficult to pick up sufficient speed to join the new road safely.

Understand the rules of dual carriageways

To do this, you need to be aware of

- the MSM and PSL routines (see page 30)
- the various speed limits that may be used on dual carriageways
- advance warning and information signs and how you should respond to them
- what you should do if your vehicle breaks down, including the use of your hazard warning lights and warning triangles
- the rules relating to motorways, some of which may also be relevant to dual carriageways
- how the weather can affect driving on dual carriageways – for example, when it's wet you need to increase your stopping distance and be aware that spray from other vehicles may affect visibility.

When can I use the right-hand lane?

On some dual carriageways the lane on the right may be used for traffic turning right as well as for overtaking. If you're overtaking, watch for clues that traffic ahead of you is slowing down to turn right.

Can you overtake on the nearside of another vehicle?

You shouldn't normally overtake on the left, but you can if the traffic is moving slowly in queues and the queue in the right-hand lane is moving more slowly.

Tips from the experts

If there's no slip road, join as you would on any other road. If you're turning right onto a dual carriageway, make sure that the central reservation is deep enough to protect your vehicle. If it isn't, you'll have to wait until the carriageway is clear in both directions before you start to cross.

When travelling on a dual carriageway at the national speed limit, remember that situations can change very quickly – use your mirrors frequently so that you always know what's happening around you.

What to expect on test

If possible, your examiner will take you onto a road where the national speed limit applies, and watch to make sure that you join the road safely. Use your mirrors effectively, and take account of the higher speed of traffic around you.

If you have to use an emergency phone, stand so that you're facing the traffic on your side of the road. You need to be able to see traffic as it approaches.

Recap questions

Q1 *Which lane should you normally drive in when travelling on a dual carriageway?*

Q2 *If you break down on a dual carriageway, how far away from your vehicle should you place a warning triangle?*

Accompanying driver advice	p100

Keep a record

Notes

Your instructor should keep a record of your progress on your *Driver's Record*. You may also like to fill in your progress below and make any notes that might help you in this space.

1 ✓	3 ✓	5
introduced	prompted	dd/mm/yy

2 ✓	4 ✓	
full instruction	seldom prompted	independent

References	HC r137–138, 173, 274	DES s8

Pedestrian crossings

You should be aware of the basic rules that apply to all pedestrian crossings but you also need to know the differences between each type of crossing.

> You need to be able to do the following **consistently** and **without any help:**

 Safely negotiate different types of crossing

To do this, you need to deal confidently with these types of crossing

- **crossings controlled by lights** – pelican, puffin and toucan crossings

- **zebra crossings** – which have no lights controlling them

- **school crossing patrols** – these aren't always at marked crossings

- **split crossings** – this includes crossings that are staggered and those that have a central refuge.

Remember, it's illegal to park on a crossing or on the zigzag lines on either side of the crossing. It's also illegal to overtake the vehicle nearest the crossing.

 Understand the rules for dealing with pedestrian crossings

To do this, you need to be aware of

- the importance of effective scanning further down the road

- how to recognise the different types of crossing from their visual characteristics

- how you should apply the MSM and PSL routines (see page 30)

- the correct speed at which to approach the crossings and the rules concerning overtaking near crossings

- when you need to stop for pedestrians who are waiting to cross

- the times and places where there's likely to be high risk; for example, near schools

- the effect that different weather conditions have on your ability to see and stop safely.

Can I wave to let a pedestrian know they can cross?

You should never wave pedestrians across in front of you as you could lead them into danger. Let them decide for themselves when it's safe to cross.

What should I look for when I'm approaching a crossing?

Watch out for pedestrians walking close to crossings, especially zebra crossings, as they may start to cross without looking at the traffic.

Tips from the experts

Make sure that you approach all crossings at a speed which allows you to stop safely if you need to.

As you approach a zebra crossing, make sure that you're aware of all pedestrians who may be intending to use the crossing.

Be patient when you're waiting at a crossing. Don't try to hurry those who are crossing by revving your engine, sounding your horn or edging forward.

If you're waiting in a queue of traffic, don't straddle a crossing. Hold back, as someone may want to cross before you're able to move off. At a controlled crossing, the lights might change.

What to expect on test

Your examiner will watch carefully to take account of how you deal with pedestrian crossings during your test. This includes how you prepare on the approach to crossings even when you don't have to stop to let pedestrians cross.

Recap questions

Q1 *Which type of crossing has a flashing amber phase, and what does it mean for you as a driver?*

Q2 *What do the zigzag lines at a crossing mean?*

Accompanying driver advice | **p101**

Keep a record

Your instructor should keep a record of your progress on your *Driver's Record*. You may also like to fill in your progress below and make any notes that might help you in this space.

| 1 ✓ introduced | 3 ✓ prompted | 5 dd/mm/yy |
| 2 ✓ full instruction | 4 ✓ seldom prompted | independent |

Notes

References | **HC** r191–199 | **DES** s7

51

Turning the vehicle around

To turn your vehicle around, it's often easiest and safest to use a roundabout or reverse into a side street. However, if these options aren't available, you may need to turn in the road.

You need to be able to do the following **consistently** and **without any help:**

 Safely turn your vehicle around in the road

To do this, you need to be confident performing this manoeuvre on

- a narrow or wide road – try not to touch the kerb at the end of each part of the manoeuvre

- a flat road or one with a camber – make sure that you don't hit the kerb

- all appropriate types of road – choose a quiet road where you have a good view in all directions.

Remember, always start to turn your wheels in the opposite direction just before you stop. Don't steer while the car is stationary – this is called dry steering and can damage your tyres and steering.

 Understand what affects how you turn in the road

To do this, you need to be able to

- observe carefully all around throughout the manoeuvre, especially checking your blind spots

- coordinate the hand and foot controls so that your vehicle moves smoothly

- steer in the correct manner while turning as tightly as possible

- use your judgement to perform this manoeuvre accurately

- avoid becoming a danger or obstruction to other road users – don't take too long to complete the turn

- choose a place to turn that's safe, legal and convenient, where you have plenty of room and there's no obstruction in the road or on the pavement.

What if the road is narrow?

Depending on the width of the road, how difficult your vehicle is to steer and the length of your vehicle, you may need to move forward and backwards several times to complete the turn.

Do I need to use the parking brake?

You may need to use the parking brake to prevent the car from rolling forward or backward if there's a pronounced camber or slope on the road.

Turn to the right and then briskly to the left just before you stop.

Turn to the left and then briskly to the right just before you stop.

Straighten up and make sure that you stay on your side of the road.

Tips from the experts

Check the road is clear in both directions before you start to move across.

The key is to keep the vehicle moving slowly while steering briskly.

What to expect on test

This manoeuvre is no longer tested on driving tests taken in England, Scotland and Wales. However, your instructor should still teach you how to turn the car around; it's a valuable skill you will need throughout your driving career.

Recap question

Q1 *What might you damage on your car if you turn the steering wheel while the car is stationary?*

Accompanying driver advice	p102

Keep a record

Your instructor should keep a record of your progress on your *Driver's Record*. You may also like to fill in your progress below and make any notes that might help you in this space.

1 ✓ introduced
3 ✓ prompted
5 dd/mm/yy independent
2 ✓ full instruction
4 ✓ seldom prompted

Notes

References	**HC** r200	**DES** s9

Reversing

You should be able to reverse smoothly and safely while under complete control. This includes reversing to the left and right around sweeping curves and sharp corners.

> You need to be able to do the following **consistently** and **without any help:**

 Safely reverse your vehicle under full control

To do this, you need to be confident reversing

- around a left and a right corner – including square and gently curved corners as well as on the straight
- on a level road and on a gradient
- on a narrow or wide road
- on a flat road or one with a camber
- on all appropriate types of road – try to choose a quiet road where you have a good view in all directions.

Remember, you can undo your seat belt while you're reversing if it interferes with your driving. Don't forget to do it up again as soon as you've finished the exercise.

Understand what affects how you reverse

To do this, you need to be able to

- find a place that's safe, legal and convenient and use your judgement to reverse accurately
- coordinate your hand and foot controls so that your vehicle moves smoothly
- steer in the correct manner while keeping reasonably close to the kerb without hitting or mounting it
- make use of effective all-round observation throughout the time you're reversing
- avoid becoming a danger or obstruction to other road users – don't take too long to complete the manoeuvre
- take account of the front of the car swinging out if you reverse around a corner.

Where should I look when I'm reversing?

Look mainly out of the back window, but don't forget to check all around throughout the time you're reversing and particularly at the point you start to turn.

How far should I aim to be from the kerb?

Keep parallel and reasonably close to the kerb all the time you're reversing.

The 'stop on the right-hand side of the road' manoeuvre. Follow the steps from 1 to 4.

Tips from the experts

As you reverse, keep a good lookout for traffic and pedestrians. Get someone to guide you if you can't see clearly.

What to expect on test

Your examiner will ask you to carry out one exercise using reverse gear. It may be the 'stop on the right-hand side of the road' manoeuvre or a reverse parking exercise (see pages 56–58). For the 'stop on the right-hand side of the road' manoeuvre, you'll be asked to stop on the right-hand side of the road, reverse for two car lengths and rejoin the traffic (see diagram).

Your examiner will watch to make sure that you reverse under full control, keeping reasonably close to the kerb. They'll assess your observation and responses to other road users.

Recap questions

Q1 *How would other road users know that you intend to reverse?*

Q2 *Into what type of road should you not reverse?*

Accompanying driver advice	p103

Keep a record

Notes

Your instructor should keep a record of your progress on your *Driver's Record*. You may also like to fill in your progress below and make any notes that might help you in this space.

1 ✓ introduced	3 ✓ prompted	5 dd/mm/yy
2 ✓ full instruction	4 ✓ seldom prompted	independent

References	HC r200–203	DES s9

Parking

Whether you're parking at the side of the road or using a bay in a car park, you need to gain the skills to do this safely before you drive on your own.

You need to be able to do the following **consistently** and **without any help:**

 Safely reverse your vehicle into a parked position

To park at the side of the road or in a parking bay, you need to be able to

- coordinate your hand and foot controls well, so that your car moves smoothly whether on level ground or on a slope

- steer in the correct manner, keeping a reasonable distance from other vehicles

- observe carefully all around while you're manoeuvring

- use your judgement to perform this manoeuvre accurately, signalling where it's necessary

- avoid becoming a danger or obstruction to other road users – don't take too long to complete the exercise.

 Understand how you should park your vehicle

To do this, you need to be aware of

- the need to check all around for other road users to make sure that you can reverse correctly and safely – don't just rely on your mirrors

- how to steer correctly – always try to steer when your car is moving. Avoid steering harshly while the car is stationary.

Remember, you need to choose a place to park that's safe, legal and convenient. You can check these in The Highway Code.

Starting position *The position you start from is important. Pull up parallel with and reasonably close to the vehicle in front of the parking place. Position your car level with or slightly ahead of the parked vehicle.*

Intermediate stages *You should be able to reverse into the space behind the parked vehicle, within the space of about two car lengths. Make sure that you don't hit the kerb while you're doing this.*

Finishing position *Before you finish manoeuvring, make sure that your car is reasonably close to and parallel with the kerb.*

Reverse into a parking bay: two options. Follow the steps from 1 to 3.

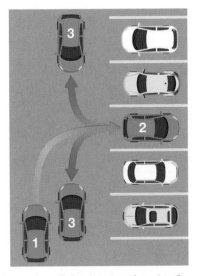

Forward park and reverse out to the left or right: two options. Follow the steps from 1 to 3.

Tips from the experts

When parking in a bay, there may be times when the layout would make it easier to turn first so that you can back into the parking space.

What to expect on test

Your examiner will ask you to do one manoeuvre involving reversing. This may be the 'stop on the right-hand side of the road' manoeuvre (see page 55) or a reverse parking manoeuvre. If you're asked to reverse park, it could be either

- a parallel park at the side of the road, or
- parking in a bay, either
  - driving forwards into a parking bay in a car park and reversing out to the left or right, or
  - reversing into a parking bay at the test centre. If you do this at the start of the test, you'll then drive away. If you do it at the end of the test, you won't be asked to drive out again.

Your examiner will tell you which manoeuvre to do, and when.

see page 55

Recap questions

Q1 *Give examples of road markings that indicate you mustn't park at any time.*

Q2 *What's the minimum distance you should park away from a junction?*

Accompanying driver advice   p104

Keep a record

Your instructor should keep a record of your progress on your *Driver's Record*. You may also like to fill in your progress below and make any notes that might help you in this space.

| 1 ✓ introduced | 3 ✓ prompted | 5 dd/mm/yy |
| 2 ✓ full instruction | 4 ✓ seldom prompted | independent |

Notes

References   **HC** r202, 238–252   **DES** s9

Emergency stop

Effective scanning and reading of the road ahead will cut down the risk of having to make an emergency stop. If it's unavoidable, brake as quickly as possible while keeping the car under full control.

You need to be able to do the following **consistently** and **without any help:**

 Safely stop your car as quickly as possible

To be able to do this while keeping full control, you need to know

- how to coordinate the brake and clutch pedals so that the car comes to a halt under full control

- the effect of ABS brakes – you need to know how to tell whether the car you're driving has ABS brakes, as this might affect the way you use the brake and clutch

- how different road and weather conditions can affect the way you stop safely

- how to control a skid if one occurs

- how to move away safely again after you've made an emergency stop.

Remember, although you need to know how to stop safely in an emergency, it's important that you know how to avoid having to do so by using your hazard perception skills to plan ahead. You should always drive in such a way that you're aware of situations that might develop and have time to respond to them safely.

Look for this symbol on your dashboard. It should light up when you turn on the ignition.

What should I do if my car starts to skid?

If you don't have ABS brakes, first release the pressure on the brake pedal. If the rear of the car starts to slide sideways, steer gently in the same direction as the skid.

How do I know whether the car I'm driving has ABS?

There will be a warning light on the dashboard and advice will be given in the handbook. Also, ask your instructor to demonstrate how ABS works.

Tips from the experts

React quickly, keep both hands on the wheel and try to stop in a straight line without allowing the car to swing off course.

Know the car you're driving – if the car has ABS brakes, make sure that you've read the handbook and know what to do, as advice can differ between manufacturers.

If you have to do this on your test, don't try to anticipate the signal that the examiner will give you.

What to expect on test

You may not have to do this exercise on your test, but if you do, your examiner will ask you to pull up at the side of the road. They'll explain the exercise and show you what the signal will be.

Before giving the signal to stop, your examiner will check the road behind to make sure it's safe. When you're given the signal, try to stop the car as you would in a real emergency.

Recap questions

Q1 *What happens if the wheels lock?*

Q2 *In what conditions would ABS brakes not work as effectively as they would normally?*

Accompanying driver advice   **p105**

Keep a record

Notes

Your instructor should keep a record of your progress on your *Driver's Record*. You may also like to fill in your progress below and make any notes that might help you in this space.

| **1** ✓ introduced | **3** ✓ prompted | **5** dd/mm/yy |
| **2** ✓ full instruction | **4** ✓ seldom prompted | independent |

References   **HC** r117–120   **DES** s5

Independent driving

Driving independently gives you the chance to experience what it will be like to drive after you've passed your test. You can acquire this key skill while learning, so that you're ready to drive alone.

You need to be able to do the following **consistently** and **without any help:**

Drive independently

To do this confidently while keeping full control, you need to

- plan ahead so that you don't have to make any late actions
- be able to follow sat-nav directions and direction signs
- use the MSM and PSL routines (page 30)
- position your car correctly in good time
- understand the correct use of lanes, both with and without directional information
- respond correctly to other road users
- know and respond to traffic signs and road markings.

Remember, you won't be prompted when to begin the MSM/PSL routine. Plan well ahead and start the routine in good time.

Tips from the experts

Look and plan well ahead. Give signals in good time but not too early or you may mislead other road users, especially if there's another turning before your junction.

If you realise you're taking the wrong turning, don't make a sudden change of direction, as this could cause a collision. It's better to complete the turn safely and then find somewhere safe to turn around and rejoin your route.

What will happen if I go off route?

If you take a wrong turning, keep calm. Your examiner will guide you back onto the original route and make sure that you know where you're expected to go.

How will I know where to turn?

Your examiner will supply a sat-nav and set the route. You have to follow the directions given by the sat-nav. One in five driving tests won't use a sat-nav; you'll have to follow traffic signs instead.

What to expect on test

This part of the test will last around 20 minutes.

Most candidates will be asked to follow directions from a sat-nav provided by the examiner.

The examiner will supply the sat-nav and set the route, so it doesn't matter what make or model of sat-nav you use while you're practising.

If you're not sure where you're going, you'll be able to ask the examiner to explain again. It won't matter if you go the wrong way unless you make a driving fault.

One in five driving tests won't use a sat-nav; you'll need to follow traffic signs instead.

Recap questions

Q1 *How do I know when to start driving independently?*

Q2 *Will I be told which lane to use?*

Accompanying driver advice	p106

Keep a record

Your instructor should keep a record of your progress on your *Driver's Record*. You may also like to fill in your progress below and make any notes that might help you in this space.

1 ✓ introduced
2 ✓ full instruction
3 ✓ prompted
4 ✓ seldom prompted
5 dd/mm/yy independent

Notes

References	HC r170–190	DES s7

Darkness

There are many factors that make driving in the dark more hazardous. Judging speed at night can be difficult, so be particularly careful at junctions.

You need to be able to do the following **consistently** and **without any help:**

 LEVEL 5 Drive safely in darkness on all types of road

To do this, you need to be confident on

- **urban roads** – the variety of different lights, such as vehicle lights, street lights and shop signs, can be distracting

- **rural roads** – the main source of light will be your headlights

- **single and dual carriageways** – there may be a mixture of lighting on these roads.

LEVEL 5 Understand the effects of darkness

To do this, you need to be aware of

- how darkness affects your visibility and therefore your speed and stopping distance, especially in bad weather

- when you need to use your lights, which lights to use and the importance of keeping them clean

- the rules concerning the use of your horn at night

- how to park safely and legally when it's dark.

The instrument panel will light up when you turn your lights on.

Remember, even within the range of your lights you can't see as clearly as you would during daylight. Pedestrians, especially those wearing dark clothing, can be difficult to see.

What do I do if a headlight stops working at night?

You should fix any lighting fault immediately, both for your own safety and for the safety of others. Don't forget to carry a spare set of bulbs with you, if appropriate for the vehicle.

What should I do if I'm dazzled by oncoming headlights?

Try not to look directly at the oncoming headlights – slow down and stop if it's necessary. Don't retaliate by leaving your headlights on full beam to dazzle the oncoming driver.

You should always use headlights in the dark, even when you're driving in built-up areas.

Tips from the experts

You should always drive so that you can stop safely within the distance you can see to be clear. At night, this means within the range of your lights.

Your lights are there to help you to be seen by others as well as to help you see. Make sure that you switch your headlights on in good time as it starts to get dark, and that you don't switch them off as it gets lighter until you're sure it's safe.

When following or meeting other vehicles, dip your headlights so that they don't dazzle other drivers.

Judging speed and distance at night can be difficult. Be particularly careful at junctions.

What to expect on test

If conditions require it, your examiner will watch to make sure that you

- use your lights correctly
- drive so that you can stop safely within the distance you can see to be clear.

Recap questions

Q1 *At night, when can you park on the side of the road without any lights?*

Q2 *When mustn't you use your horn at night?*

Accompanying driver advice   p107

Keep a record

Your instructor should keep a record of your progress on your *Driver's Record*. You may also like to fill in your progress below and make any notes that might help you in this space.

| 1 ✓ introduced | 3 ✓ prompted | 5 dd/mm/yy |
| 2 ✓ full instruction | 4 ✓ seldom prompted | independent |

Notes

References   **HC** r112–115, 248–252   **DES** s13

Weather conditions

You need to be aware of the effect some weather conditions, such as fog and low sun, can have on visibility. Other conditions, such as ice, snow and rain, can affect the way that your vehicle handles.

You need to be able to do the following **consistently** and **without any help:**

Drive safely in all weather conditions

To do this, you need to be confident in these weather conditions

- **fog** – remember, fog is often patchy, so your level of visibility can change very quickly
- **ice and snow** – check weather forecasts and only travel if it's absolutely necessary
- **bright sunshine** – be aware of the glare this may cause, especially when the road is wet or the sun is low
- **wind** – you may be affected by gusts of wind around buildings, bridges, etc
- **rain** – wet roads mean longer stopping distances. Your visibility may be affected by spray from other vehicles.

Understand how to deal with weather conditions

To do this on all types of road in urban and rural areas, you need to be aware of

- how different weather conditions will affect your visibility, speed and stopping distance. You need to demonstrate that you can respond to these conditions safely
- how the condition and characteristics of your vehicle can affect its handling
- the warning signs and signals that may be used
- how to avoid skidding and aquaplaning, and how to control them if they do occur
- when to use your lights and which lights to use in poor visibility.

Remember, when the roads are wet, your stopping distance may be doubled. In icy conditions you may need to allow 10 times the normal stopping distance.

Be aware that after heavy rain, the water level in a ford is likely to be much higher than normal.

Ford

What if it becomes foggy?

Slow right down; it's much more difficult to judge distances and the speed of other vehicles in fog. Use dipped headlights – and fog lights when visibility is seriously reduced.

What do I do if the road is flooded?

Stop and assess how deep the water is. If the water's not too deep, drive on slowly. Remember to test your brakes afterwards.

Tips from the experts

Always keep your windscreen, mirrors and windows clean and clear, so that you can see as much as possible all around.

You may not be affected by high winds, but be aware that other road users, such as cyclists, motorcyclists and drivers of high-sided vehicles, are more vulnerable and may be blown into your path.

When visibility is reduced by fog, use dipped headlights and, if the distance you can see falls below 100 metres (328 feet), use your front and rear fog lights. If you do use fog lights, remember to switch them off when visibility improves.

It's not only bad weather that can cause difficult driving conditions. The glare of the sun – especially when the sun is low in the sky in winter – can make it very difficult to see other road users.

What to expect on test

Your examiner will watch to make sure that you drive according to the weather conditions prevailing during the test.

Recap questions

Q1 How can you tell that you're aquaplaning, and what should you do to regain control?

Q2 Why is it dangerous to leave your rear fog lights on if conditions improve?

Accompanying driver advice   **p108**

Keep a record

Your instructor should keep a record of your progress on your *Driver's Record*. You may also like to fill in your progress below and make any notes that might help you in this space.

| 1 ✓ introduced | 3 ✓ prompted | 5 dd/mm/yy |
| 2 ✓ full instruction | 4 ✓ seldom prompted | independent |

Notes

Environmental issues

Everything from the type of car and its fuel consumption to the way in which you drive influences the environment. You need to understand how to minimise the negative effects.

> You need to be able to do the following **consistently** and **without any help:**

 Understand how driving affects the environment

To do this, you need to be aware of

- **air pollution** – the effect that vehicle exhaust gases have on the climate, your health, and the health and safety of others. Understand the beneficial effect of catalytic converters on the environment
- **noise pollution** – try to avoid making unnecessary noise, especially when travelling at night or in residential areas.

It's illegal to pour oil down the drain *– you need to dispose of it correctly.*

 Minimise your effect on the environment

To do this, you need to know how you can

- change your driving style so that you cause less damage to the environment
- maintain your vehicle in a good condition to make it run more efficiently
- dispose of vehicle waste such as spent oil, old batteries and used tyres correctly
- reduce your fuel consumption by limiting your use of air conditioning and removing any unnecessary load
- use the highest possible gear without making the engine struggle.

Remember, many of the suggestions for reducing environmental impact will also reduce your motoring costs.

Does my speed really affect my fuel consumption?

Yes, it makes a big difference. If you travel at 70 mph (112 km/h), you're likely to use up to 30% more fuel than if you covered the same distance at 50 mph (80 km/h).

Does the car I buy make a big difference?

Try to choose a vehicle with low fuel consumption. For further information about fuel and carbon-dioxide emissions, check **www.gov.uk**

Tips from the experts

Use your hazard perception skills to plan ahead, so that you can avoid harsh braking and acceleration. Driving smoothly can reduce your fuel consumption by about 15%, as well as reducing the wear and tear on your vehicle.

Reverse into a parking space so that you can drive out of it. Manoeuvring when the engine is cold uses lots of fuel. Don't over-rev your engine in a low gear.

Check tyre pressures regularly. Incorrect tyre pressure results in a shorter tyre life and may be dangerous. Under-inflated tyres can increase fuel consumption.

Try to avoid using your car for very short journeys, especially when the engine is cold. Also, consider car-sharing or using public transport where you can.

Avoid carrying unnecessary weight and remove a roof rack when it's not being used. The drag on a roof rack can increase fuel consumption by up to 15%.

What to expect on test

You'll be asked questions that test your understanding of environmental issues during your theory test.

Recap question

Q1 *Why are catalytic converters fitted?*

Accompanying driver advice   p109

Keep a record

Your instructor should keep a record of your progress on your *Driver's Record*. You may also like to fill in your progress below and make any notes that might help you in this space.

1	3	5
✓	✓	dd/mm/yy
introduced	prompted	independent

Notes

References   **HC** r123   **DES** s17

Passengers and loads

As a driver, you need to understand the responsibilities that you have to any passengers, whether they're adults or children, and also how to secure any items that you're transporting.

You need to be able to do the following **consistently** and **without any help:**

 Carrying passengers and loads safely

To do this, you need to know

- your responsibility as a driver regarding carrying passengers (other adults, children and babies) and animals in your car safely
- the safest way to carry loads in and on your car
- how to load trailers safely and carry bicycles on your car.

 Understand the rules of carrying passengers and loads

To do this, you must be aware of

- the rules concerning the use of seat belts, especially when you're responsible
- the importance of not putting a rear-facing baby seat into a seat that's protected by an airbag
- the importance of checking that all doors are shut properly and that animals are safely restrained in a purpose-made carry box or behind a guard
- how to stow luggage or load it securely and the importance of distributing weight evenly.

Remember, don't overload your car with passengers. Ensure that everyone is wearing a seat belt before you start.

What do I do if a trailer I'm towing starts to swerve?

Try to avoid this happening by distributing the weight properly in the trailer. If it does happen, ease off the accelerator to reduce speed gently.

Can I tow a trailer without taking another test?

You can tow a small trailer under 750 kg maximum authorised mass without having to take another test. You may also be able to tow a larger trailer (see pages 131–139).

Tips from the experts

Specially designed roof boxes are streamlined so they'll save fuel as well as securing the load safely.

Special cycle racks fitted on top of or behind the car allow you to carry cycles securely. If they're fitted behind the car, make sure that the number plates and lights can still be seen clearly.

If you're carrying a load, make sure that it's secure and that it doesn't stick out dangerously.

Any load will have an effect on the handling of your car – changes to the weight and centre of gravity will affect the steering and braking. Allow more stopping distance when you're carrying a heavy load. You may also need to inflate your tyres more and adjust your headlights (see your vehicle handbook).

What to expect on test

You'll be asked questions about passengers and carrying loads during your theory test.

Recap questions

Q1 *Who's responsible for ensuring that children under 14 wear a seat belt?*

Q2 *What's the speed limit for a car towing a trailer travelling on a single carriageway road?*

As the driver, *you're responsible for ensuring that any baby or young child is wearing an appropriate restraint.*

Accompanying driver advice   p110

Keep a record

Notes

Your instructor should keep a record of your progress on your *Driver's Record*. You may also like to fill in your progress below and make any notes that might help you in this space.

1 ✓	3 ✓	5 dd/mm/yy
introduced	prompted	independent

References   **HC** r99–102   **DES** s2

Security

This covers not only the security of your vehicle but also its contents and your personal security. You need to be aware of the ways in which you can reduce the risks.

You need to be able to do the following **consistently** and **without any help:**

 Understand the importance of personal safety

To do this, you need to be aware of

- the need to stay alert at all times
- the importance of letting someone know where you're going and when you expect to arrive or return
- why you shouldn't leave important or valuable items on display in your car
- the need to choose a sensible place to leave your car, especially at night.

Remember, if possible, park your car in an attended or secure car park. For information and to search for approved sites, visit parkmark.co.uk

 Understand the importance of vehicle security

To do this, you must be aware of

- how to find a safe place to park
- the different security measures available, such as steering-wheel locks and immobilisers.

A steering-wheel lock is one of the measures you can use to improve the security of your vehicle.

When should I lock away my valuables?

Criminals could be observing your actions in the car park. Try to lock valuables away before leaving home.

Where can I get advice about vehicle security?

Speak to your local crime prevention officer, who will advise you on devices and any vehicle watch schemes that may operate in your area.

71

Tips from the experts

An alarm or immobiliser, a visible security device such as a steering-wheel lock or having the registration number etched on all the windows can deter a would-be thief.

Before you leave your car, make sure that you remove all valuables (or at least lock them out of sight), close all the windows and then lock the doors.

If you have to park on the side of the road at night, leave your car in a well-lit area.

Carry a mobile phone so that you can use it to call for help if you break down, are involved in an incident or feel threatened in any way.

Always lock your car even if it's for a short time, such as when paying for petrol.

What to expect on test

You'll be asked questions about vehicle security during your theory test.

Recap question

Q1 *What measures can you take to protect your personal safety when parking at night?*

Accompanying driver advice   **p111**

Keep a record

Notes

Your instructor should keep a record of your progress on your *Driver's Record*. You may also like to fill in your progress below and make any notes that might help you in this space.

1 ✓ introduced
3 ✓ prompted
5 dd/mm/yy independent

References   **HC** r239, p131   **DES** s20

Learning to drive on the motorway

Learner drivers can have driving lessons on motorways but only with an approved driving instructor (ADI) and in a car fitted with dual controls that's clearly displaying L plates. However, motorway driving isn't part of the practical driving test. The Highway Code has specific rules about motorway driving (r253–273), though many of the other rules apply to motorway driving too.

Your ADI will be able to tell you when you're ready to take lessons on the motorway. It's recommended that this only takes place near to the end of your training, when you're ready to take your practical driving test. You should be competent and in full control of the vehicle, and also know the requirements of motorway driving.

Topics to be covered include:

- joining and leaving motorways, using acceleration and deceleration lanes
- effective use of mirrors
- planning and effective observation
- awareness of other road users
- lane discipline
- separation distances
- reactions to signals, road signs and markings
- how to avoid fatigue, journey planning and use of service areas
- overtaking
- dealing with other vehicles, side winds and turbulence
- smart motorways, active traffic management (ATM)
- dealing with contraflow and other road maintenance
- accident and breakdown procedures
- safe use of the hard shoulder.

Remember, motorways are the safest of our roads as only 4% of crashes happen on motorways and account for just 5% of all fatalities. When they do occur, however, they tend to be serious because of the speeds involved.

73

section **three**

ACCOMPANYING DRIVER ADVICE

This section covers

- Accompanying a learner
- Getting started
- Attitude
- Planning
- Legal responsibilities
- Cockpit checks
- Safety checks
- Controls and instruments
- Moving away and stopping
- Safe positioning
- Mirrors – vision and use
- Signals
- Anticipation and planning
- Use of speed
- Other traffic
- Junctions
- Roundabouts
- Dual carriageways
- Pedestrian crossings
- Turning the vehicle around
- Reversing
- Parking
- Emergency stop
- Independent driving
- Darkness
- Weather conditions
- Environmental issues
- Passengers and loads
- Security

Accompanying a learner

When accompanying a learner, look on the process of making your relative or friend a safe driver as a team effort involving you, your learner and their ADI.

If you feel unsure about anything or want a bit of advice, you can talk to the ADI about the areas that concern you. You may want to accompany your learner on their next lesson to see how the ADI copes with situations you find difficult. Make sure that your learner is happy for you to sit in and arrange a suitable time with the ADI.

Sometimes the ADI may teach a driving technique that seems wrong to you. Remember, as cars become

more sophisticated, so recommended techniques change to take advantage of new technology.

The ADI is probably using the most up-to-date methods, which may be different from the way you were taught. Don't confuse your learner by expecting them to do things 'your way'. One part of your role is to enable your learner to practise the techniques taught by their ADI.

> **Remember,** working together is the best way of ensuring everyone's aim of safe driving for life.

Getting started

Beginning

For a new driver, there's an awful lot to learn. The list includes

- a good knowledge of driving theory
- learning how to operate a complicated set of controls (which looks so easy)
- operating the controls while putting the theory into practice
- developing good judgement
- anticipation and awareness.

As well as developing these skills, the new driver needs to learn to cope with

- other road users
- the weather
- road conditions
- navigation.

> **Remember,** new drivers can't begin driving until they've received their licence from the Driver and Vehicle Licensing Agency (DVLA) and it has come into effect.

Even after basic control skills have developed, being able to cope with constantly changing demands and unexpected events – often in a fraction of a second – is a skill that comes with experience.

The whole business is complicated, challenging and, for some, extremely difficult. To expect that all this can be learned in a few short lessons is a mistake.

A learner driver needs to gain enough skill and experience to enable them to drive alone safely once they've passed their driving test. As more miles are driven and more experience is gained, the novice driver will gradually progress towards becoming an experienced driver.

However, driving is a subject where there are always new lessons to be learned and it's a foolish and dangerous driver who thinks they know it all.

So how does a learner begin the process of going from novice to competent safe driver? The answer lies in two key areas

Training – to learn new skills

Practice – to gain experience.

Training

Most people learn to drive with an ADI. Driving instructors are professionals who are trained to teach driving skills in a structured manner to suit differing abilities.

Remember, some insurance companies don't insure people under 25 years of age, while others may offer reduced premiums for new drivers who complete the Pass Plus scheme (see page 128).

Don't risk driving uninsured!

Many pupils only have one or two hours of professional driving instruction each week and their experience is often limited to driving at the same time of day and over the same types of road.

Four levels of learning to drive

1 **Unconscious incompetence**
We don't know that we don't know

Ignorance

2 **Conscious incompetence**
We know that we don't know

Take driving lessons

3 **Conscious competence**
We do it but we have to concentrate really hard

Practice The hard part is going from 3 to 4 without getting dejected

4 **Unconscious competence**
We do it so naturally we can think about other things at the same time

Awareness and anticipation

Danger of overconfidence

Where you fit in

As an accompanying driver, you'll be helping your learner have more practice and gain wider experience of the varied driving conditions they're likely to meet once they've passed their driving test.

However, there are a few things to consider before you start (see below).

Once you're ready to take on this responsibility, you need to think about developing the skills of your learner – know their limits and don't attempt any driving that will be beyond their ability.

You're helping a new driver to gain skills that will help to keep them safe for many years to come.

That's not to say it will be an easy task. There may be times when you need to remind yourself why you're there.

Don't forget that only an ADI can charge for driving lessons. Even accepting money for fuel is an offence unless you're an ADI. Don't be caught out.

> **Remember,** learners who combine extra practice with professional lessons not only perform better on their driving test but go on to have a reduced incident rate in the early years of driving unaccompanied.

Can you do it legally?

Before you agree to accompany a learner driver, there are a few things you need to check.

1 Have you held a full EC/EEA driving licence for at least three years for the category of vehicle being driven?

2 Are you at least 21 years of age?

3 Is the car you intend to use insured for use by the learner?

4 Is the car fitted with L plates (D plates in Wales) to both the front and rear of the car?

5 Is the car you intend to use in a safe, roadworthy condition?

The answer must be YES to all questions before you can act as an accompanying driver to a learner.

What can you expect?

To start with, don't expect this to be easy. Learning to drive takes a lot longer than most people realise. You need to set aside plenty of time for practice sessions in order to develop your skills properly.

If you set dates and times when you're expecting to go out with your learner, you're more likely to be in a calm frame of mind than if you've had to stop what you were doing and grudgingly give your time.

Be guided by the ADI, but once the basic skills have been learned, it's a good idea to let your learner do a lot of the everyday driving, such as to the shops or to school or college.

If your learner struggles with something you think is easy, don't worry. Everyone learns at different rates and in different ways, and it may be necessary to go over the same ground many times.

The memory often plays tricks and you may have forgotten how you struggled with some aspects of learning to drive.

Remember, young drivers are about twice as likely as older drivers to be involved in a road traffic incident when negotiating a bend.

What are you expecting to achieve?

The goals you should be helping a new driver to achieve are

- confidence and competence in practising these new skills

- a sound basis on which to build their driving career

- enough experience to be able to think for themselves and cope safely with any driving situation they meet

- confidence about their ability to pass the driving test

- an understanding of their responsibility as a driver.

Some learners struggle with the clutch, while others have difficulty with the gears. The key is to be patient.

The practice vehicle

Is your car suitable for your learner to drive? A learner may learn in any make or model of car, but a large, powerful car may be more difficult to control than a smaller model.

Small cars aren't necessarily any easier to drive but their size can make judging the car's position easier, especially during manoeuvres.

It might be helpful to find a driving school that uses a similar car to your own. If this isn't possible, make allowances for your learner if they struggle to adapt to your car after lessons in the school car.

Make sure the L (or D) plates are secure. You don't want them to fly off once you try roads with higher speed limits.

Remember, fit an extra rear-view mirror. Knowing what's going on behind is important for safety and peace of mind.

L plates – Avoid fixing L (D) plates to the windscreen or rear window, since they restrict the view. Don't forget to cover or remove the L (D) plates when the car is being used by a full licence-holder.

Attitude

Bad habits

It's too easy for bad habits to creep unnoticed into anyone's driving. Before you act as an accompanying driver, it's worth looking at your own driving. You'll have little credibility if you expect your learner to drive one way while you practise another – and don't expect your learner not to notice. Why not have a lesson or two with the ADI yourself? This will allow an expert to check your driving and help you to improve your skills.

Drinking and driving, speed limits, use of signals, seat belts and attitude to other road users are all aspects of driving where standards slip. Setting a good example when you drive will have positive benefits for both you and your learner.

Patience

Frustration can soon set in when your learner struggles with something you think should be easy, or can't do something that they could do the last time you went out. If something is proving difficult, don't keep trying it until tempers fray. Leave it and come back to it another time. Learning to drive should be an enjoyable experience, not an ordeal.

Other road users may be inconsiderate and show little regard for the fact that your driver is a learner. Don't allow this to wind you up, since it will also affect your learner. Knocking a learner driver's confidence can ruin their driving career before it has even started.

Technique

Before accompanying your learner, you should give some thought to how you're going to

- give directions
- cope with dangerous situations.

Remember, learning to drive takes a lot longer than most people think. Be patient with your learner.

Your learner will need clear directions given calmly and in plenty of time. You'll need to look and think that bit further ahead than normal. If your learner has difficulty telling their right from their left, you'll need to overcome this problem. Your ADI should be able to give you some advice on these matters, as well as tips on giving directions at any complex junctions in your area.

Safety is your priority. Where possible, you should act early to prevent hazards from developing into dangerous situations. If a dangerous situation does develop, you may need to

- speak firmly and clearly without shouting
- reach across and take control of the steering
- use the handbrake
- use dual controls if fitted.

Avoiding conflicts

Accompanying a novice driver can be frustrating, unnerving and a lot harder than you think. Here are a few points worth remembering to help you keep on top of it.

- Talking to the ADI will help you plan practice sessions which avoid areas that are too difficult for your learner's present level of ability.

- Learn from mistakes and don't dwell on them. Encouragement and tolerance will help skills and confidence develop.

- Nothing is achieved if you allow yourself to become angry with your learner. If it's all going wrong, have a break for five minutes or stop the session altogether if things are too bad.

- If something happens which scares either of you, pull over and give yourselves time to calm down. Discuss what went wrong and why. Were you expecting too much from your learner?

- If another road user fails to show your learner due consideration, don't allow it to upset you. Set a good example, keep calm and turn the experience into a lesson in anticipation.

> **Remember,** keep reminding yourself that you're making a big difference to your learner's long-term driving safety. Learners rarely have crashes while practising.

- Prevent your learner from getting into difficulties by looking well ahead so you can anticipate problems. Don't expect them to have the same degree of awareness and judgement as you.

- Your learner is going to drive in the way their instructor has taught. If any techniques differ from the way you drive, don't argue over who's right or insist they do it your way. Make a note and discuss it with the ADI.

Planning

When to start

DVSA recommends that new drivers reach a level of proficiency with an ADI before starting to practise with an accompanying driver. Ask the ADI to tell you when your learner is ready to start practising. Starting too soon may be unnerving for both of you and could lead to anything from a loss of confidence through to a serious loss of control.

> **Remember,** a learner driver may find driving very tiring. Many crashes involving young drivers result from lack of experience.

Use the *Driver's Record* to see the progress being made and the topics needing practice. To start with, this will mostly be control skills, but it will gradually move on to include the whole syllabus.

Early days

Before you begin your first practice sessions, you need to give some thought to where and when you're going to conduct them. When you begin, driving in heavy traffic at rush hour isn't going to be good for either of you.

Where Pick a quiet area where

- there won't be much traffic to deal with
- you won't cause a nuisance to other road users or local residents.

It's also a good idea to find somewhere fairly level because of the added difficulties a hill can create at this stage.

Your learner will probably drive quite slowly and, despite your efforts to find somewhere quiet, you may find a queue of traffic building up behind. If this happens, be prepared to ask your learner to pull over somewhere safe and let the traffic pass.

When Plan the first few practice sessions to avoid busy times of the day. These include rush hours, school start and finish times, and during local events.

Your learner can only practise when you make the time available. Work and other commitments may make demands on you and the only time you have could be evenings and weekends.

In the winter months, evening practice will be in the dark – but don't let this be an excuse not to practise. As long as the weather conditions aren't dangerous, practising in the dark shouldn't be a problem.

During Remember that you're in charge of the vehicle even when the learner is driving. You need all your concentration for supervising the learner – you **MUST NOT** use your mobile phone or other hand-held device at any time while the provisional licence-holder is driving a motor vehicle on a road (see page 19).

Planning your sessions

Many learners take their driving lessons at the same time of day and drive repeatedly on the same types of road.

> **Remember,** could your learner cope with any situation that might arise? They'll have to when they pass their test.

While this may provide a level of familiarity with these roads, it does little to provide a broad experience of the wide variety of driving conditions your learner will meet when they've passed their test.

Good practice sessions should build both experience and confidence. This can be achieved by planning each session around your learner's requirements and their driving limitations. Refer to their *Driver's Record* to see which topics need practising.

As part of your planning, you'll need to think about routes, time of day, road types, manoeuvring and weather conditions. These are now looked at in turn.

Routes Thinking through where you're going to take your learner will enable you to

- avoid areas that may have features such as a steep hill or a difficult junction which they're not yet ready to encounter
- practise certain aspects, such as left turns, traffic lights, one-way streets, etc.

You don't want to put your learner into a situation that they can't cope with and which could have been avoided if you'd planned ahead.

Time of day Local knowledge will tell you which roads are busiest and when. This will allow you to avoid the worst areas in the early days, and practise in heavy traffic when your learner is ready.

Daylight, dusk and darkness are driving conditions that require different skills, which need to be practised. If your learner has great difficulty seeing at night, have their night vision tested by an optician. Your learner should be able to think independently and use the car's lights when necessary.

Road types Unless you're an ADI, you can't accompany a learner driver on the motorway (see page 73). You can help them to practice on all other types of road. If a Driver's Record is being used, it will indicate the types of road where practice is needed.

Manoeuvring The driving test requires manoeuvres that reflect real driving situations to be demonstrated. These include stopping in an emergency, turning the car around in the road, reversing into a side road and parking using reverse gear, both on the road and into car-park bays.

The ADI will teach the techniques and, if a *Driver's Record* is being used, will record which have been taught and which need practice.

Weather conditions Many learners begin learning in the spring months and pass their driving test before winter arrives.

These learners may have had little or no experience of driving in

- rain and slippery conditions
- mist and fog
- windy conditions.

These are everyday conditions that most motorists encounter in their first year of driving. When the ADI indicates your learner is ready to cope with them, be prepared to go out in these conditions as they occur.

> **Remember,** don't underestimate the weather. Extreme weather can make driving unsafe. It's recommended that you avoid practising in these conditions in the early days.
>
> If in doubt – don't venture out.

Key skills

The following pages (86–113) give advice and tips on helping your learner to practise the 25 key skills explained in section 2.

Legal responsibilities

Refer to   p22

At **Level 5**, your learner should have a full understanding of their legal responsibilities as a driver. These include

- driving licences and accompanying learner drivers
- vehicle tax (SORN), insurance and MOT
- health and eyesight
- New Drivers Act
- tiredness and rest periods
- traffic rules and regulations
- alcohol and drugs
- mobile phones
- vehicle condition
- dealing with road traffic incidents.

Remember, ignorance is no excuse in the eyes of the law. Make sure that you're both up to date.

How you can help

Ask questions so that your learner has to think about their responsibilities. If you're both unclear about an issue, then work together to find out the facts. For example, if you didn't know about the New Drivers Act, you could ask your ADI to explain it to both of you.

To keep up to date with changes in the law, own and refer to the latest edition of The Highway Code. For example, new rules have been introduced that make it an offence to smoke in a private vehicle if there's a passenger under 18 in the car. It's the driver's responsibility to enforce this law (see **www.gov.uk** for details).

What to expect

Many new drivers will have an understanding of the issues that directly affect them, such as applying for a driving licence. They may not know about recent changes in the law or matters that you routinely deal with, such as taxing your car.

If you involve your learner, they may not only learn the processes but they may also appreciate the costs associated with owning and running a car.

Cockpit checks

Refer to p24

Your learner will have reached **Level 5** for this topic when they independently

- make a point of checking their door is closed properly
- check and, if necessary, adjust their driving position. This includes adjusting the seat, steering wheel, head restraint, etc
- correctly fasten their seat belt
- check and adjust the mirrors
- check the handbrake is on and the gear lever is in neutral.

How you can help

Watch to see that your learner completes their checks before starting the engine. Look to see that each item is checked and not just mentioned.

What to expect

It's not uncommon for learners to find that, once they're on the road, one or more mirrors require some further adjustment, or the seat needs repositioning.

Don't let them try to make adjustments while on the move. Find a safe place for them to pull over and stop before making any further adjustment.

> **Remember,** mirrors need to be adjusted so that they can be used with the least possible head movement.

Safety checks

Refer to **p26**

As part of their driving test, your learner will be asked to show and explain basic safety checks necessary to keep their car safe on the road.

The ADI will cover the driving-test requirements but learning how to carry out routine safety checks isn't something to learn for the test and then forget. Aspects such as tyre condition are the driver's responsibility. If the tyres are illegal, the driver could be fined or have penalty points added to their driving licence.

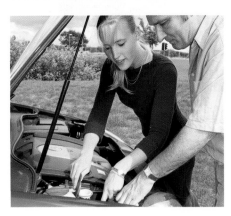

How you can help

Before each practice drive, watch while your learner carries out safety checks on your vehicle. Developing a habit of regular checks can also help identify faults at an early stage and this may prevent the vehicle from breaking down during a journey.

Allowing your learner to clean the windscreen, windows, mirrors and lights will help you and will also help them to remember these aspects.

What to expect

Many new drivers don't have an interest in the workings of the car but they do need to understand

- daily and weekly vehicle checks
- service intervals
- MOT requirements.

The importance of having your vehicle regularly serviced should be stressed. You could show your learner how you keep a record of your car's service intervals.

Remember, 'POWER'

P Petrol
O Oil (engine oil and brake fluid)
W Water (engine coolant, windscreen washers)
E Electrics (lights, indicators)
R Rubber and brakes.

Controls and instruments

Refer to p28

Reading and understanding instruments such as the speedometer and the fuel and temperature gauges is essential.

By the time your learner is ready for their test, they should also understand the warning lights and, importantly, know what action to take if one comes on while they're driving.

In the early days of learning to drive, controlling the steering, gears and foot controls will take all your learner's concentration. As their skill develops, it's also important for them to become competent with ancillary controls such as the demister, wipers, heaters, etc.

> **Remember,** your learner should be able to operate all the controls without looking down to find them.

How you can help

Allow your learner to familiarise themselves with the layout of the controls and instruments, and explain any special features that may be fitted to your car.

The controls may be laid out differently in the ADI's car and this could lead to some confusion; for example, if the windscreen wiper controls are on the left of the steering column instead of on the right.

What to expect

When you're in situations that call for the use of certain controls, such as the front or rear screen demister, your learner may be concentrating really hard on their driving and fail to realise the need to use them.

Don't allow the situation to become dangerous, but do encourage your learner to recognise for themselves when these controls should be used.

If your learner fumbles while trying to find and operate the control they want, pull up somewhere safe and run through the control layout again.

Moving away and stopping

Refer to   p30

Choosing a safe place to stop and stopping safely are things that every driver needs to do. Your learner will also need to develop sound judgement and awareness of other road users.

How you can help

While your learner is having to concentrate really hard on using the controls, they may forget to watch for other road users. Stay alert and don't let them move off into danger. Practise moving off

- on level ground
- uphill
- downhill
- from behind a parked vehicle.

Asking your learner to pick somewhere safe to stop will allow them to think for themselves. They need to look for somewhere to stop and then use their mirrors and signals correctly while bringing the car to rest at their chosen place. When teaching someone to stop, you should advise that a gear change isn't always necessary.

What to expect

Every time your learner moves off, expect them to go through a lengthy process of finding the biting point and balancing the accelerator and clutch against the handbrake. This will make moving off a slow process and this, in turn, makes dealing with road junctions more difficult.

Frustration may set in as

- traffic builds up behind
- your learner can't pull out into a space that you would find safe as a driver.

If you find your learner has difficulty with busy junctions, avoid them and pick quieter alternatives until the necessary control skills have developed.

When stopping, watch that your learner doesn't try to stop suddenly without allowing time for using the mirror and signalling if necessary. Use the extra rear-view mirror to check the traffic behind you.

> **Remember,** traffic lights are one place where tension can build. When the red light changes, it's not uncommon for novices to stall in their rush to move off promptly. This can lead to panic, especially if there's a queue of traffic behind. Stay calm and don't react to another driver sounding their horn – they may not be able to see the L plates if they aren't immediately behind.

Safe positioning

Refer to | p32

With experience, judging the car's position becomes second nature, but learning to position accurately is a surprisingly difficult skill to learn.

Some learners look just in front of the car, rather than well ahead. This makes it more difficult to judge the car's width and position on the road. As well as the control skills, your learner will need to know

- where to position the car for any particular driving situation
- the meaning of signs and road markings.

How you can help

The skill of being able to judge the car's position on the road from the passenger seat will develop with practice. You may need to reach across and steer into the correct position. Try to remain calm and don't allow the wrong road position to go uncorrected for any length of time.

At first, avoid using places such as narrow streets or roads with width restrictions until your learner has developed a little in both confidence and skill. Then you can move them onto areas and roads requiring more accurate judgement.

What to expect

Before your learner's judgement has developed, they may

- drive too close to the kerb, the edge or centre of the road, parked cars, or other obstructions
- position the vehicle poorly around bends and junctions
- show poor lane discipline.

Don't allow your learner to hit the kerb while driving normally. The impact may wrench the steering wheel from their grasp, causing serious loss of control. It may also damage or burst the tyre.

Some mistakes can be scary for you as a passenger but your learner may be unaware of this, or that they've made an error. If it's going wrong, pull over and talk about it. You may need to demonstrate their mistake in order for the learner to realise it for themselves. If you disagree on positioning, then discuss it with the ADI.

Mirrors – vision and use

Refer to   p34

The ADI will cover this subject early in the learning process but watch for your learner having to make exaggerated head movements to use the mirrors. This may mean adjustments are needed, once you've stopped in a safe place.

Correctly adjusted mirrors give a good view behind and to the sides of the car. It's important that your learner uses the mirrors when necessary and is aware of the areas not covered by the mirrors (and that they know how and when to check them).

How you can help

When accompanying your learner, look to see if they're checking the mirrors correctly. If a mirror check is missed, you should always draw their attention to it, but avoid prompting them too early – they may become reliant on your prompt rather than thinking for themselves.

Don't let them change direction without first checking that it's safe.

To check if your learner is using their mirrors, fit another small interior mirror on the left of the windscreen, angled so that you can see your learner without having to look directly at them.

> **Remember,** when turning right in busy traffic, there will be occasions when a blind-area check to the right needs to be made in case a vehicle is attempting to overtake. There may be so much else going on that this check is missed and you may need to make it on their behalf.

What to expect

When watching your learner's use of mirrors, check

- how well they time their mirror checks
- that they act correctly on what can be seen.

You may find yourself having to look and plan further ahead than normal, so that you can identify hazards early enough to then be watching to see how your learner deals with them. This can have an extra benefit in that it improves your own hazard awareness.

Signals

(Refer to   **p36**)

Drivers need to know how and when to give signals and the meaning of signals given by others. Whichever way signals are given, they must be given clearly and in good time. Your learner must be able to identify the signals of others and act correctly on them.

How you can help

Watch your learner's use of signals and make sure they only use signals shown in The Highway Code. Try to use routes that will expose your learner to the need to think about the timing of a signal or whether a signal is appropriate; for example

- when passing a parked car with a road junction on the right

- turning right or left when there's another junction just before your turn.

If in any doubt about the correct procedure, ask the ADI for advice.

What to expect

In the early part of their training, learners will be thinking about their use of the car controls and may forget to signal. This may be dangerous; for example, when pulling up while being followed by another vehicle. Remain alert and give help in good time if safety is threatened.

There may be occasions when another road user gives a signal that your learner hasn't met before, such as reversing lights on a car that's trying to reverse park into a space on the side of the road.

Learners tend to shy away from using the horn. However, it's a valuable aid to road safety when used correctly and you should encourage its use when appropriate.

Most indicators will automatically cancel after a manoeuvre, but sometimes they might not. Don't let an uncancelled signal continue for any length of time – it could mislead another road user and lead to danger.

> **Remember,** the horn must only be used while the vehicle is moving, to make other road users aware of your presence. Refer your learner to The Highway Code.

Anticipation and planning

Refer to   p38

Before your learner can react to a risk, they must perceive that a risk exists. That perception is governed by

- training (in this situation, do this)
- experience (I've met this before and need to do this)
- planning (what should I do now to prevent risk in the situation I can see?)
- anticipation (what if?).

One of the main problems for inexperienced drivers is that they don't recognise the hazard until it's too late to avoid the danger.

How you can help

Practice is so important. During practice, your learner will meet situations that they've never met before. While you're sitting next to them, your experience in both seeing and reacting to any risk should keep them safe and, where possible, you can pass on the benefit of your experience.

While your learner can never experience every type of hazard, you can aim to instil in them a heightened awareness of hazards and a knowledge of how to cope with them.

What to expect

Your learner may feel they have everything under control, but if the way they deal with hazards makes you feel uncomfortable, something is wrong with their driving. When a mistake has been made, you'll need to highlight the potential danger in their response to a situation.

Learners can be defensive about their driving ability and you should take account of their feelings. Stay calm and don't raise your voice, but do make sure they understand the consequences of their actions.

> **Remember,** new drivers often don't look very far ahead. They can be too slow to identify potential danger and don't realise how soon they need to react.
>
> Step in to help before danger develops.

Use of speed

Refer to   p40

Driving too fast is one of the main causes of road traffic incidents on all types of road. Driving too slowly is a different mistake and one that creates its own set of hazards.

So how fast should your learner be driving? What's a suitable speed? The answer is dependent on a number of variables and getting it right takes practice.

Your learner must never drive beyond their ability or the speed limit, but they'll need to become able to drive on all roads without hindering the flow of traffic.

How you can help

The more experience your learner has of various driving situations, the better they'll become at assessing the correct speed for different conditions and reacting to changes in the speed limit.

If your learner is timid, remember that they may take a long time to feel confident about making progress.

If you think your learner isn't improving very quickly, don't be negative or critical – a timid driver needs encouragement, not criticism. Learning to drive is a lengthy process, so you'll need to allow more time for practice.

Don't ignore rural roads where wide variations in speed can be experienced, as this will be good practice for your learner. In these rural areas, they'll have to

*   plan ahead
*   continually adjust their speed.

Remember, make sure that your learner obeys speed limits and understands that the limit isn't a target – it's the maximum speed that's legally permitted.

It isn't always safe to drive at the speed limit.

What to expect

You can expect your learner to start by driving slowly in all situations. In particular, expect very slow acceleration up through the gears, which can make emerging at junctions difficult and, for you, frustrating.

For the first few practice sessions, don't let your learner drive the car if you're in a hurry to get somewhere, as this may make you feel impatient.

If you become critical and negative, what sort of message do you think this gives your learner about correct driver behaviour towards other road users?

You need to be patient, tolerant and understanding. As experience and confidence grow, speeds will increase and skills in hazard awareness and planning ahead will develop. However, overconfidence and an irresponsible attitude towards risk need to be discouraged.

The ADI will teach learners how to keep a safe distance from the vehicle in front, but the learner must then put this theory into practice when they drive. Help them practise applying the two-second rule appropriately and safely until it becomes a habit.

It's vital that your learner understands that they're responsible for the consequences of their driving behaviour.

Other traffic

Refer to   p42

Your learner needs to gain experience in dealing with traffic while having the safety net of an experienced driver sitting by their side. While you can't cover every possible situation, you should be able to help them learn to deal safely with

- meeting oncoming traffic
- turning across the path of other vehicles
- overtaking
- parked vehicles or other obstructions.

How you can help

These traffic situations call for judgement and often there's little or no room for error. Don't allow your learner to overestimate their own ability or their car's performance. If they make a mistake, you're there to prevent it from developing into something more serious.

Avoid busy main roads until confidence has developed. Find places to practise that include

- narrow roads
- parked cars and other obstructions
- roads with right-turn lane markings
- traffic lights
- box junctions.

As well as practising dealing with obstructions on your side of the road, find places where your learner has to anticipate the actions of an approaching driver who might not give way. For hazards that you don't encounter, you can always talk to your learner about possible situations. Thinking about potential danger is a big part of developing hazard awareness.

> **Remember,** you're responsible for ensuring that your learner doesn't create dangerous situations through inexperience or poor judgement.

What to expect

Learners will usually be cautious; on busy roads you may wait for some time. Don't become frustrated if you feel that some opportunities are being missed – as confidence builds, so will ability.

When waiting to turn right, you may find oncoming drivers will give way and invite your learner to turn. Before accepting, your learner must check for other road users, such as motorcyclists and cyclists.

When overtaking, many mistakes can be made through inexperience and lack of judgement.

Errors can include

- overtaking too slowly
- overtaking when the vehicle in front is driving close to the speed limit
- not allowing enough room
- cutting in too soon after overtaking.

Also remember that, if your car is different from the ADI's, your learner may take time to get used to judging its width.

When meeting oncoming traffic, your learner needs to judge the available space and, if necessary, give way.

Junctions

Refer to   **p44**

Dealing with junctions includes driving straight ahead as well as turning right and left. Junctions can be any shape or size, including those with

- road markings
- no road markings
- traffic lights
- warning signs.

Your learner will have to learn where and when they should be looking and what they're looking for. Interpreting what they see and planning how to deal with the possible outcomes is a skill that develops with experience.

Your learner should already be familiar with the signs and markings in The Highway Code, but they first have to see the sign or marking and realise how it affects them before they can act on the information given.

> **Remember,** don't be fooled by your learner's apparent confidence – their hazard perception skills won't be well developed, even though they think they're observing well and feel everything is under control.

It's important to explain the importance of assessing whether another road user has seen you when dealing with junctions – it may take a while for them to develop this ability.

Correctly timed signals help other road users to know your learner's intentions.

How you can help

Refer to the *Driver's Record* to see which level your learner has reached and plan their practice accordingly.

Try to find junctions where you can practise turning into as well as out of side roads, or one where your learner can drive round a circuit or block.

When planning a location, consider whether

- there will be much traffic
- both turns and emerges can be practised
- there are road markings to help with positioning
- there are any difficulties; for example, steep slopes or poor visibility at any of the junctions.

What to expect

The ADI will already have covered the Mirrors – Signal – Manoeuvre routine for dealing with junctions. However, new learners may be struggling with steering or changing gear while thinking about speed, mirrors, road position and signs.

Remember, if your learner isn't confident in their ability to move off, they may try to emerge from a junction without stopping to see if it's safe. If you can't see that it's safe, neither can they.

Don't let them cause an incident.

In addition, new drivers often don't look very far ahead and may not see, or may misjudge, any approaching traffic. They can also be slow to identify potential danger.

Mistakes can easily happen and a mistake at a junction can be dangerous as well as frightening for both of you. If you can't see that it's safe, then neither can your learner. Keep calm and step in to help before any danger develops.

Roundabouts

Refer to   p46

Many learners find it difficult to cope with roundabouts. The ADI may ask for them to be practised in stages, eg turning left, turning right and going ahead. If that's the case, you'll need to plan routes accordingly.

Try to include a variety, from large multi-lane roundabouts to small and mini-roundabouts.

> **Remember,** rear-end collisions are very common at roundabouts. They're often caused when a driver waiting to join the roundabout doesn't do so but the driver behind expects them to have moved. The driver behind then moves forward while looking for traffic on the roundabout, without checking whether the car in front has continued to move forward. Be aware of this hazard at busy roundabouts.

How you can help

When you're approaching a roundabout, tell your learner in plenty of time which direction you want them to go. If possible, use other instructions to help them, such as 'follow the sign to the town centre' or 'the third exit'.

If your learner becomes disorientated, tell them in good time where their exit is, to allow them time to position correctly.

If they miss the exit, don't worry. Direct them round again, using the appropriate lane or road position and take the exit required. You need to encourage your learner to plan their route onto, around and off the roundabout. Try to avoid a situation where your learner is part-way around the roundabout before they start to think about which road they should be taking.

What to expect

If your learner is uncertain of the direction they're supposed to be going, expect incorrect signalling and positioning. They may also

- drive too slowly, which can cause problems if there's fast-moving traffic
- veer suddenly to take an exit at the last moment, with no thought for other traffic.

Learners often struggle with directions on roundabouts. Try to get them to make use of the signs, so that they know what to expect.

Dual carriageways

Refer to   p48

Dual carriageways aren't governed by the same regulations that apply to motorways.

However, driving at higher speeds and in lanes on a dual carriageway is valuable experience both in itself and in preparation for motorway driving.

How you can help

As well as driving in the correct lane on the dual carriageway, your learner needs to gain experience of

- using slip roads
- turning right
- overtaking
- high-speed traffic.

Gaining such experience during adverse weather conditions, in twilight and during the hours of darkness is also very valuable.

What to expect

Most learners begin by driving relatively slowly, and this is fine when driving along a dual carriageway. However, joining a dual carriageway from a slip road can call for firm acceleration. If your learner isn't too confident with accelerating through the gears, wait until the skill has developed before attempting to join a dual carriageway.

When overtaking, your learner will need to judge the length of their vehicle accurately. If they don't, there's a danger of cutting in too soon as they return to the left lane.

Remember, vehicles ahead may want to turn right through the central reservation. Don't let your learner confuse their right signal and positioning in the right-hand lane as a sign that they're overtaking, when other clues (such as brake lights or a junction sign) show that they may be turning right.

Pedestrian crossings

| Refer to | p50 |

There are laws governing pedestrian crossings that your learner must know and with which they must comply. There are also several types of pedestrian crossing – do you know them all?

How you can help

When your learner is approaching a crossing, see if they can tell you which type of crossing it is and which rules apply.

Going out for a drive at school start and finish times should ensure plenty of opportunities to deal with busy crossings.

Darkness adds another aspect to safely dealing with pedestrian crossings, so practice during twilight or the hours of darkness is also recommended.

What to expect

Noticing there's a crossing ahead is the first hurdle. You'll soon tell if your learner hasn't spotted it, and you may need to act promptly. However, don't let your learner over-react and stop unnecessarily. This could cause a danger to traffic behind you.

Make certain that they understand the sequence of lights at light-controlled crossings, and react correctly to each phase of the lights.

> **Remember,** pedestrians are among the most vulnerable road users. If you have any doubts about your learner's ability to cope, give assistance until you're happy that they can cope unaided and without any risk of losing control.

Turning the vehicle around

Refer to   p52

The skills required to turn the car around in the road will be needed every time your learner has to manoeuvre in a confined space.

How you can help

You may wish to familiarise yourself with the technique taught by the ADI. This is explained in detail in *The Official DVSA Guide to Driving – the essential skills*. When looking for a place to practise the exercise, consider

- road width
- visibility
- traffic volume
- local residents.

Be courteous to other road users while your learner is practising. Be prepared to find somewhere else if the first place turns out to be less suitable than you first thought.

What to expect

Some learners can take time to recall techniques they've been taught – panic may set in and disorientation may follow halfway through an exercise. They might struggle with the controls, fail to notice other road users or be unable to judge the car's length. Be supportive and offer encouragement, rather than criticism, if it's all taking longer than you anticipated.

You may temporarily release your seat belt while your pupil is carrying out a manoeuvre that involves the reverse gear, to give a little more freedom in which to teach the exercise safely. However, you **MUST** refasten it once the manoeuvre has been completed.

> **Remember,** a sudden loss of control when turning can cause the vehicle to surge forwards or backwards onto the pavement and collide with whatever is in the way. You'll need to act promptly if your learner loses control in this manner.

Turn to the right and then briskly to the left just before you stop.

Turn to the left and then briskly to the right just before you stop.

Straighten up and make sure that you stay on your side of the road.

Reversing

Refer to   p54

For many learners, reversing accurately is the most difficult part of learning to drive. If your learner finds reversing difficult, you can expect to spend a lot of time practising this skill.

How you can help

It's easier to begin by practising reversing into a junction on the left, rather than one on the right. The techniques for both are described in *The Official DVSA Guide to Driving – the essential skills.*

Look for a place to practise where

- there's good visibility
- the road is level
- you don't expect much traffic
- you won't annoy local residents.

A crossroads or staggered junction isn't a suitable location to practise reversing. Don't just use one location but try to find a variety of junctions for practice sessions.

What to expect

Reversing doesn't come easily to many learners. If your learner becomes despondent, move on to another topic and return to reversing practice another day.

Practising on an uphill slope before skills have developed is likely to cause wear on the clutch and noise as the engine is excessively revved. Try to avoid this until your learner has developed some skill and confidence in reversing on flat ground.

Remember, good all-round observation is essential when reversing.

Modern cars have exterior mirrors fitted on both sides of the car. If these mirrors are used for reversing, remember that

- there's no view directly behind the car
- the driver may focus solely on the detail seen in the mirror and fail to see other road users or obstructions
- the mirrors aren't set for rear observation when driving. There are still blind spots that need to be checked by looking around.

Parking

Refer to — p56

On their driving test, your learner may be asked to demonstrate their ability to park in a bay in a car park or in a space behind another parked car on the side of the road. See pages 56–58 for details of the driving-test requirements.

> **Remember,** whether parking in a car park or on the roadside, your learner should be able to position the car accurately, confidently and safely. You must ensure that your learner doesn't hit another vehicle while they're practising.

How you can help

When practising reverse parking on the side of the road, your learner will inevitably cause a temporary obstruction to any traffic flow. For this reason, choose a quiet location for practice.

To practise parking in a parking bay, you'll need to find a suitable car park where your learner can practise this manoeuvre. Avoid busy car parks and peak times of day. Try to find a parking bay that has an empty bay on either side, which will allow a greater margin for inaccurate steering. While your learner's vehicle control skills are developing, you can help by being their eyes and ears, watching out for other road users. As car control develops, you can let them become responsible for the safety aspects themselves.

As with other reverse manoeuvres, don't allow your learner to rely only on the car's mirrors while reversing.

What to expect

Parking calls for accuracy, control and judgement. Your learner may be weak in any or all of these skills. When they set about reverse parking on the side of the road, you can expect them to have trouble judging where to pull up in readiness to reverse into the space. This may result in pulling up too close alongside, or too far past, the parked car, or perhaps not far enough forward past the parking space.

If your learner misjudges the car's length when reversing into a parking bay, they may go beyond the edge of the bay, or into a wall or barrier, causing damage to your car.

To park on the roadside, your learner should pull up reasonably close to and parallel with the vehicle in front.

Make sure that your learner doesn't hit the parked vehicle and is aware of passing traffic.

The car should be parked within the space of about two car lengths, close to and parallel with the kerb.

Emergency stop

Refer to p58

Practising stopping the car as if there were an emergency provides valuable experience in reacting quickly and correctly while controlling the car under emergency conditions. Practising what to do in an emergency is the only way to help your learner to cope if a real situation ever arises.

Remember, relying on your additional interior mirror to tell you what's behind isn't enough.

How you can help

Find somewhere with very little traffic, a good road surface, and where screeching tyres won't cause a nuisance. Agree with your learner the signal to give and begin practising at low speeds. Only progress to higher speeds when your learner has gained sufficient control skills to cope. Also, make sure that you look around carefully before giving any signal to stop.

What to expect

The ADI will have given instruction in the use of the controls. If your vehicle has an anti-lock braking system fitted, there may be special instructions on how to achieve maximum braking. Be prepared for your learner to use excessive force when applying the brakes, which may cause

- skidding, accompanied by loud screeching and smoke from the tyres
- a severe jolt that could cause injury to your back or neck.

On giving the signal, brace yourself and prepare for a sudden rapid deceleration.

Independent driving

Refer to **p60**

Learning to drive independently is an important part of preparing your learner

- for their driving test
- to drive after they've passed their driving test.

On their driving test, a learner will be asked to drive independently for around 20 minutes. Most candidates will be asked to follow directions from a sat-nav provided by the examiner. The examiner will supply the sat-nav and set the route, so it doesn't matter what make or model of sat-nav you use while you're practising. One in five driving tests won't use a sat-nav; the learner will need to follow traffic signs instead.

Learner drivers can come to rely on the direction they're given as a prompt to begin the MSM/PSL routine. If you remove the step-by-step directions, they'll need to think for themselves and plan ahead, exactly as they will when driving unaccompanied.

Remember, at first your learner may be unsure where to go, especially at complicated junctions. Give them help if they need it, but as they're approaching their driving test they should be thinking for themselves.

How you can help

To help your learner drive independently, you'll need to give them some practice at following directions from a sat-nav. You can also ask them to follow the directions shown on road signs and give them the opportunity to think for themselves.

What to expect

At first, they may be so focused on thinking about the directions that they forget to signal or are late moving into the correct lane or road position. They may also overlook other important features, such as traffic lights, pedestrian crossings or road markings. You should be ready to step in if necessary. Once they start to think for themselves and plan ahead, they'll be better prepared for driving after their test.

Darkness

Refer to **p62**

Your learner needs to practise driving in the dark since this calls for a new set of skills. As well as knowing how and when to use the car's lights, they have to learn how to cope with

- poor visibility when light levels are low
- glare from the lights of other vehicles
- not dazzling other road users.

How you can help

Try to give your learner as much experience as possible of driving in the dark on a range of roads, such as well-lit urban roads, unlit rural roads and dual carriageways. When driving in the dark, show your learner

- how to use the anti-dazzle mirror, if your car has one fitted
- how and when to dip the main-beam headlights to avoid dazzling others.

When driving on rural roads without footpaths, ask them to think about pedestrians.

- Where should they be walking?
- What if they're wearing dark clothing?

Could your learner cope?

Make sure they check The Highway Code for advice and rules on driving, parking, vehicle lighting and use of the horn at night.

What to expect

The bright lights of oncoming traffic can be difficult to cope with. If an approaching driver has forgotten to dip their headlights, your learner may be dazzled and unable to see the road ahead. Don't let them

- continue without reducing speed
- retaliate by using their headlights to dazzle the approaching driver.

Don't forget that vulnerable road users such as cyclists, pedestrians and motorcyclists may be very difficult to see in the dark.

Many people adapt easily to driving in the dark, but others find it very tiring. If your learner finds it tiring, be ready to end the practice session and take over the driving yourself.

Remember, in busy urban areas, lights from shops and street lamps can make it easy to miss traffic lights, crossing lights, vulnerable road users, etc. You're responsible for making sure that no mistakes are made.

Weather conditions

Refer to p64

Adverse weather conditions such as fog, frost, high winds and rain are all common driving conditions.

In more severe weather conditions of snow and ice, be guided by the advice of local travel experts to determine whether conditions are suitable for your learner.

How you can help

If the conditions aren't severe, you should take opportunities for your learner to practise when possible. In bad weather, your learner needs to pay attention to how the conditions affect their

- speed and ability to stop
- use of windscreen wipers/demisters
- need to use dipped headlights.

Explain that, just because they may think they can see adequately during the day in dull, foggy or wet conditions, this doesn't mean their vehicle can be seen clearly by others. If in doubt, use dipped headlights for safety and visibility until conditions improve.

What to expect

Driving too close to the vehicle in front is a common mistake. Make sure that the two-second rule is used, and that the gap is increased if conditions will affect the stopping distance. Front or rear fog lights may be used if fitted, but make sure they're turned off if conditions improve.

Also remember that anti-lock brakes (ABS) don't replace the need for good driving skills. ABS prevents wheels from locking, so that steering control is retained, but vehicles can still skid because of ice, surface water or a loose road surface. Make sure that your learner fully understands this.

Environmental issues

Refer to   p66

Your learner needs to understand that they can reduce exhaust emissions by driving in an environmentally friendly manner. They'll save money by using less fuel, and they'll improve their hazard awareness skills by looking and planning further ahead.

How you can help

The ADI should be able to explain the recommended driving techniques, which can also be found in *The Official DVSA Guide to Driving – the essential skills*. Encourage your learner to practise these techniques.

Keeping a check on fuel consumption will show you the effect that driving in an environmentally friendly manner can have. This may encourage you to adopt these techniques yourself.

To help your learner appreciate environmental issues other than fuel consumption, talk about

- the importance of good maintenance, and keeping tyres correctly inflated
- disposal of oil, old tyres and batteries.

Remember, harsh use of the accelerator and heavy braking significantly increases fuel consumption.

What to expect

Learners tend to drive more slowly than experienced drivers until their confidence builds. You can help your learner to understand that careful use of speed and an awareness of fuel consumption will help them continue to drive in an environmentally friendly manner. Encourage them to keep doing so.

Passengers and loads

Refer to   **p68**

Your learner must understand the driver's responsibility when carrying passengers. They must be aware of the latest seat-belt regulations, details of which are in The Highway Code.

They must also understand the effect that a load can have on a vehicle's handling/braking and the importance of not overloading their vehicle. Help your learner develop good awareness of their responsibilities to prevent them from breaking the law.

How you can help

Letting your learner drive with passengers can be a valuable experience. If any are under 14 years, the driver is responsible for ensuring that they wear a seat belt or appropriate child restraint. Make sure that

your learner is aware of this. It's also the driver's responsibility to stop anyone in the car from smoking if any passenger is under 18.

Use any opportunity to let your learner practise in a loaded vehicle; for example, when going on holiday. Discuss the way extra weight can affect the vehicle and explain the importance of making sure that the load is secure and not sticking out dangerously.

Refer to the vehicle handbook for advice on altering tyre pressures when carrying heavy loads.

What to expect

If the car is heavily loaded, its acceleration may be slower than normal. Make sure that your learner takes this into account when emerging from a side road, or moving off on an uphill gradient. Braking may also be affected – make sure that your learner understands this and recognises that they should allow themselves more time and a greater distance in which to stop the vehicle safely.

If you're carrying an animal such as a family pet in the car, it's important to keep it under control. Loose animals can be a serious distraction and could cause an incident.

> **Remember,** if the car is filled with people, there's likely to be conversation. Make sure this doesn't distract either of you.

Security

Refer to | p70

Your learner needs to be aware of the importance of security – not only of the vehicle and its contents, but also their own personal security. Information on vehicle safety can be obtained from your local crime prevention officer.

How you can help

When looking for a place to park the car, your learner may be preoccupied with the process of parking and not thinking about the security issues.

If they choose to park in a place that has a security risk, ask them whether they think they've chosen a safe place to park. If necessary, you should point out the risk. Make sure they understand the importance of not parking in poorly lit areas and not leaving any valuables on display.

If your vehicle is fitted with an immobiliser and/or alarm, make sure your learner is familiar with its operation and that they use it whenever they park the car.

If you have a high-visibility security device such as a steering-wheel lock, show your learner how to use it.

What to expect

If your learner is naturally security-conscious, they'll happily take measures that cut down the risks. If not, you may have to nag them to understand that using a car makes them a potential target for car crime; it's in their own interest to safeguard themselves and their property.

Remember, many car crimes are committed on petrol-station forecourts when the driver leaves the car to pay for fuel. Alerting your learner to the risk may prevent them from becoming a victim.

section **four**
THE TEST AND BEYOND

This section covers

- Are you ready for your test?
- Booking your practical driving test
- The day of your test
- The practical test
- Your test result
- Pass Plus
- Developing your driving skills

Are you ready for your test?

You'll be ready for your practical test when you show that you've reached **Level 5** in all the key skills listed on the *Driver's Record*, not before.

The pass rate for the practical test is about 45%. Those learner drivers who pass first time do so because they've had plenty of professional instruction and practice. Make sure you're one of them.

> **Remember,** your instructor has the knowledge and experience to tell you when you're ready. You'll be ready when you can drive consistently well, with confidence and without assistance or guidance. If you can't do this all the time, you're not ready to take your test.

Are you sure you're ready to drive on your own? Don't apply for your test too soon; wait until you're ready. It'll save you time and money.

It's important that, throughout your training, you've been learning the theory and putting it into practice when you drive – you need to do the two things in parallel. However, you'll need to take and pass a theory test before you can apply to take your practical driving test.

The theory test

There are two parts to the theory test: the first consists of multiple choice questions, and the second is a hazard perception test. Both parts are taken in the same session.

There are more than 150 theory test centres in Great Britain and Northern Ireland. Theory test sessions are available on weekdays, some evenings and some Saturdays.

It's important that you study – not just to pass the test, but to become a safer driver.

You'll usually be able to get an appointment within about two weeks (a bit longer if you have special needs).

You can find out where your local centre is from your instructor, online at **www.gov.uk** or by calling **0300 200 1122.** More information about the theory test and the multiple choice questions is given in *The Official DVSA Theory Test for Car Drivers* book or DVD-ROM.

The Official DVSA Guide to Hazard Perception DVD-ROM will help you prepare for the hazard perception part of the theory test, as well as preparing you for driving on the road.

When you pass your theory test, you'll be given a pass certificate. You have to quote the number on this certificate when you book your practical test, and you must bring the certificate with you when you take your practical test.

The theory test certificate is valid for two years. If you don't pass your practical test within that time, you'll have to take and pass another theory test before you can book your practical test.

When you drive on your practical test, your examiner will expect you to demonstrate what you learnt for your theory test.

I can't read very well, so I'm worried about taking my test

If you have reading difficulties, there's a voiceover for the test, which may help. You may also be allowed extra time in some circumstances. You can select this option when you book your test online.

How will I know what to do on the hazard perception part of the test?

Once you've done the multiple choice part of the test, and before you start the hazard perception part, you'll be shown a short tutorial video that explains how the test works and gives you a chance to see a sample clip. This will help you to understand what you're expected to do once the second part of the test starts.

Booking your practical driving test

How to book

You have all the **Level 5** boxes on your *Driver's Record* completed, you've passed your theory test and you're ready to take your practical test.

It's easiest to book your test online or by telephone. You can also book by post but only if you intend to pay by cheque or postal order.

Online or by telephone If you book by either of these methods, you'll be given the date and time of your test immediately. You can book online at **www.gov.uk**

To book by telephone, call **0300 200 1122** Monday to Friday. If you're deaf and use a minicom machine, call **0300 200 1144**. If you're a Welsh speaker, call **0300 200 1133**.

You'll need to tell the operator what sort of test you want to book and provide

- your theory-test pass certificate number
- your driver number (shown on your licence)
- your driving-school code number (if you have it)
- your credit/debit card details. Please note that the person who books the test must be the card holder.

You may be asked if you can accept a test at short notice. Ask your instructor beforehand about this if you would need to use their car. You'll be given a booking number and sent an appointment letter within a few days.

Booking by post Fill in an application form, which you can get from driving-test centres or your instructor. Send the form, together with the correct fee, to the address shown on the back of the form. Don't forget to give your preferred date when you book.

With postal bookings, you may only pay by cheque or postal order. Please don't send cash. You'll receive an appointment email/letter within 10 days.

Apply well in advance of when you want to take your test. At test centres in Wales, you can take the test in the Welsh language. Please indicate your choice when booking.

Your confirmation will be sent in the post if you don't provide an email address. If you haven't received a reply after two weeks, call **0300 200 1122**.

Disabilities or special circumstances

Whichever way you book your test, you need to say when booking if you have a disability or if there are other special circumstances. However serious your disability is, you'll still take the same driving test as every other test candidate, but more time will be allowed for the test.

This is so that your examiner can talk to you about your disability and any adaptations fitted to your vehicle. For further information, visit **www.gov.uk**

To make sure that enough time is allowed for your test, it would help DVSA to know if you

- are deaf or have severe hearing difficulties
- are in any way restricted in your movements
- have any disability that may affect your driving.

If any of these apply to you, please say so when you book your test. If you're deaf or have severe hearing problems, you're allowed to bring a signer. (This can be your instructor.) The signer must be 16 years or over.

How much does the test cost?

Your instructor should be able to tell you, or you can find out on **www.gov.uk** or by calling 0300 200 1122.

Can I take my test on a weekend or in the evening?

At some test centres, you can take a test on a Saturday or Sunday, or on a weekday evening. The fees at these times are higher than those for tests during normal working hours on weekdays. Evening tests are available during the summer months only.

How do I change or cancel my test?

You can change or cancel your test online at **www.gov.uk** or by calling the booking office on **0300 200 1122**. (You may even be able to switch to an earlier date.)

You must give at least three clear working days' notice, not counting the day DVSA receive your request and the day of the test. (Saturday is counted as a working day.) If you don't give enough notice, you'll lose your fee. (Short-notice rebooking is permitted in exceptional circumstances – see **www.gov.uk** for details.)

The day of your test

Make sure that you arrive for your test in good time and try to relax. You need to bring the correct documents with you and ensure that the vehicle you'll be driving is suitable to take out on test.

Before your test, you'll have to sign a declaration that your insurance is in order and that you meet the residency requirements.

Documents

When you arrive at the test centre, you need to have with you

- your provisional driving licence
- your theory-test pass certificate
- your valid passport, if your licence doesn't show your photograph. (Your passport doesn't have to be British.) No other form of identification is acceptable in England, Wales or Scotland. Other documents may, however, be acceptable in Northern Ireland; please check **nidirect.gov.uk/motoring**

Your examiner won't be able to conduct the test if you can't produce one of these licences

- a provisional driving licence issued in Great Britain or Northern Ireland, or a full GB or NI licence giving the provisional entitlement
- an EC/EEA licence if you want to take a test for a category not covered by your full EC/EEA licence.

If you have a full driving licence that was issued in another country but isn't eligible for exchange for a GB licence, you must have a GB provisional licence.

All documents must be original – DVSA can't accept photocopies.

Your test vehicle

Make sure that the vehicle you're going to drive during the test is

- legally roadworthy and has a current MOT test certificate if it needs one
- mechanically sound and all equipment required by law is fitted and working correctly; for example, the speedometer must show mph and km/h. In some cars, the spare wheel is a space-saver intended for temporary use only. You can't take your test if one of these is being used

- fully covered by insurance for its present use and for you to drive – your examiner will ask you to sign a declaration that your insurance is in order before you take your test.

A hire car can only be used for the driving test if it's fitted with dual controls. Any vehicle used for the test should also have

- valid vehicle tax
- L plates (or, if you wish, D plates if you're taking your test in Wales) displayed to the front and rear of the vehicle – don't fix them to the windscreen or back window as both you and your examiner should have a clear view of the road
- seat belts – make sure they're clean and work properly
- head restraints fitted ('slip-on' head restraints aren't permissible on test)
- an additional interior rear-view mirror for the examiner to use.

Can I take my test in an automatic car?

You can, but if you pass you'll only get a full licence to drive an automatic. There's sometimes some confusion about what's classed as an automatic. For clarity, vehicles with three pedals (accelerator, brake and clutch) are classed as manual; vehicles with two pedals are classed as automatics.

Remember, if you overlook any of these points, your test will be cancelled and you'll lose your fee. Make sure that your vehicle is suitable for the test well in advance.

The controls, seating, equipment and any other objects in the vehicle must be arranged so that they don't interfere with the conduct of the test. A dual accelerator (if fitted) must be removed before the test.

You won't be able to take your test if your vehicle isn't suitable; for example, if it

- has no clear view to the rear, other than by use of the exterior mirrors
- has only a driver's seat
- has more than eight passenger seats or is over 3.5 tonnes in weight
- doesn't have seat belts or head restraints fitted to the front seats
- has been subject to a manufacturer's recall but you don't have a certificate showing that the work has been carried out
- is carrying a load
- is towing a trailer (see page 131).

If you're using a left-hand-drive car, take special care and make full use of your mirrors.

Adapted vehicles

If you pass your test in a motor car that has been specifically adapted for your disability, your licence will restrict you to driving vehicles fitted with the necessary adaptations.

The practical test

You should aim to reach **Level 5** in all the key skills. Try to relax and drive as you've been driving during your lessons and practice.

Your examiner wants you to do well and will try to help you relax. If you want to talk during the test, that won't be a problem – your examiner will talk with you but might not say too much because they don't want to distract you from your driving. Don't worry if you make a mistake; keep calm and concentrate on your driving for the rest of the test. Unless it's a serious or dangerous fault, you won't fail on this unless you make the same mistake a number of times.

You'll pass if you can show your examiner that you can drive safely and demonstrate, through your driving, that you have a thorough knowledge of the rules of The Highway Code and the theory of driving safely.

Does the standard of test vary?

No, all examiners are trained to assess tests to the same standard. The test routes are designed to include a range of typical road and traffic conditions and the examiners are closely supervised to make sure they follow the national standard. A senior examiner sits in on some tests to make sure the examiner is assessing the standard of your driving properly. If this happens on your test, don't worry – they won't be looking at you, so just carry on as if they weren't there.

Can anyone accompany me on the test?

Yes, we encourage this. The examiner will ask you if you would like your instructor, or anyone else (preferably the person who trained you to drive) to accompany you on test and be there for the result and end-of-test feedback.

It can be helpful to take your instructor with you. Pass or fail, your instructor can discuss your test with you and identify any further training you might need.

Anyone who goes with you must be 16 or over and wear a seat belt, but they mustn't take any part in the test.

Your driving instructor should be preparing you to drive alone after you've passed the test, so you should already be learning the skills you need to do so and be able to make decisions for yourself. Once you've passed your test, you'll need to navigate roads safely, often dealing with distractions such as passengers and music.

Throughout the test, your examiner will be watching how you drive and how you put into practice the things you learnt for your theory test.

You must satisfy them that you've fully understood all aspects, especially

- alertness and concentration
- courtesy and consideration
- care in the use of the controls to reduce mechanical wear and tear
- awareness of stopping distances, speed limits and safety margins in all conditions
- hazard awareness
- correct action concerning pedestrians and other vulnerable road users
- dealing with other types of vehicle in the correct manner
- road and traffic signs.

The test lasts for about 40 minutes. The route will have been been selected to include as many different road and traffic conditions as possible.

Your examiner will give you directions clearly and in good time, but if you're not sure about anything, just ask. Your examiner understands that you might be nervous and won't mind explaining again.

Other elements in the test

Apart from general driving, your test will include the following elements:

Eyesight test Before you get into your car, your examiner will point out a vehicle at a suitable distance and ask you to read its number plate. You must satisfy them that you can read it, as detailed on page 10. If you need glasses or contact lenses to read the number plate, that's fine, but you must wear them during the test and whenever you drive.

If you can't speak English or have difficulty reading, you may copy down what you see.

If your answer is incorrect, your examiner will measure the exact distance and repeat the test. If you fail the eyesight test, your test will go no further.

Safety checks Your examiner will ask you

- one 'tell me' question at the beginning of your test, before you start driving. This is where you explain how you'd carry out a safety task
- one 'show me' question while you're driving; for example, showing how to wash the windscreen using the car controls (see page 26).

Special exercises You'll be asked to carry out one of three possible reversing manoeuvres

- parallel park at the side of the road (see page 56)
- park in a bay (see pages 57–58)
- stop on the right-hand side of the road (see page 55).

Independent driving All practical driving tests include approximately 20 minutes of independent driving, during which you'll be asked to drive by either

- following directions from a sat-nav, **or**
- following traffic signs towards a destination.

This part of the test will enable your examiner to assess how you manage traffic and road systems on your own, and show that you have the skills to be a safe novice driver.

For further information on this part of the test, please check the latest details at **www.gov.uk**

Your examiner will also ask you to pull up on the left several times during the test. This is to demonstrate your ability to stop and move away

- safely
- while in full control of your car.

Emergency stop You may be asked to carry out an emergency stop. (One in three tests includes an emergency-stop exercise.)

How the examiner records faults

Total   S   D

① ② ③④

Total faults ⑤

① Driving fault A less serious fault, but an accumulation of these may result in failure

② Area total The number of driving faults made in one area

③ Serious fault Committing one of these will result in failure

④ Dangerous fault Committing one of these will result in failure

⑤ Overall total The total number of driving faults made in all areas during the test

How your driving test is assessed

Your examiner is looking for evidence that you have the required skills, knowledge and attitude to be a safe driver.

Throughout your driving test, your examiner will assess your driving and will complete a report, which is used to provide you with feedback at the end of the test.

You'll fail your test if you commit a serious or dangerous fault. You'll also fail if you commit more than 15 driving faults.

The examiner will use the following criteria

Driving fault Less serious, but has been assessed as such because of circumstances at that particular time. An accumulation of more than 15 driving faults will result in failure.

Serious fault Recorded when a potentially dangerous incident has occurred or a habitual driving fault indicates a serious weakness in a candidate's driving.

Dangerous fault Recorded when a fault is assessed as having caused actual danger during the test.

Guidance after the test

After the test, pass or fail, you'll be offered feedback on your driving performance and an explanation of your driving-test report.

The Data Protection Act prevents your instructor from talking to your examiner about your practical test without your permission.

Having your instructor in the car will give them the opportunity to support your ongoing learning and development. We encourage you to let your instructor see your test and listen to the test result and feedback.

If you haven't passed, your instructor will have a better understanding of the reasons for this. They will then be able to address the specific weaknesses you've shown during the drive through further training before your next test.

If you've passed, your instructor will be better placed to advise you about your ongoing development as a new driver.

Ecosafe driving

Ecosafe driving is a recognised and proven style of driving that contributes to road safety while reducing fuel consumption and emissions.

At the end of the test, the examiner will remind you to discuss ecosafe driving with your instructor and learn how you can save money.

Your test result

If you don't pass

Your driving isn't up to the standard required. You made mistakes that could have caused danger on the road.

Your examiner will help you by

- giving you a driving-test report form. This will show all the faults marked during the test

- explaining briefly why you haven't passed.

Listen to your examiner carefully. They'll be able to help you by pointing out the aspects of your driving that you need to improve.

Study the driving-test report. It will include notes to help you understand how the examiner marks the form. You may then find it helpful to refer to the relevant sections in this book.

Show your copy of the report to your instructor, who will advise and help you to correct the faults. Listen to your instructor's advice carefully and get as much practice as you can. You can't take another test for at least 10 days.

Right of appeal You'll obviously be disappointed if you don't pass your driving test. Although your examiner's decision can't be changed, if you think your test wasn't carried out according to the regulations, you have the right to appeal. If you live in England and Wales, you have

six months after the issue of the Statement of Failure in which to appeal (Magistrates' Courts Act 1952 Ch. 55 part VII, Sect. 104).

If you live in Scotland, you have 21 days in which to appeal (Sheriff Court, Scotland Act of Sederunt (Statutory Appeals) 1981).

If you pass

Well done! You've shown that you can drive safely and confidently. Your examiner will give you a copy of the driving-test report, which will show any driving faults that have been marked during the test.

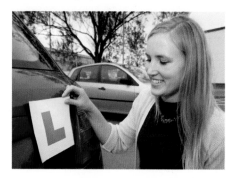

Your examiner will then ask for your provisional licence so that an upgraded licence can automatically be sent to you through the post.

Once the details have been taken, your examiner will keep your provisional licence and it will be securely destroyed. You'll be given a pass certificate as proof of success until you receive your new licence.

If you don't want to surrender your licence you don't have to, and there will be certain circumstances when this isn't possible – for example, if you've changed your name.

In these cases, you'll have to send your provisional licence, together with your pass certificate and the appropriate fee, to DVLA and it will send you your full licence. You must do this within two years or you'll have to take your test again.

Look at the test report carefully and discuss it with your instructor. It includes notes to help you understand how the examiner marks the form.

You may then find it helpful to refer to the relevant sections in this book to help you overcome those weaknesses noted during your test.

Special rules under the New Drivers Act apply for the first two years after you've passed your test.

New Drivers Act

Your licence will be revoked if you receive six or more penalty points as a result of offences you commit within two years of passing your first practical test. This includes any offences you may have committed before passing your test.

> **Remember,** you'll get a minimum of three penalty points for speeding – two speeding offences means six points.

If you wish to continue driving, you'll have to reapply for a provisional licence. You'll then have to drive as a learner until you pass the theory and practical driving tests again. This applies even if you pay by fixed penalty.

For more information, see **www.gov.uk**

Pass Plus

Pass Plus is a training scheme for new drivers. Its aim is to improve your driving skills and make you a safer driver. It can also lead to insurance discounts.

The scheme has been designed by the Driver and Vehicle Standards Agency (DVSA), with the help of motor insurers and driving instructors, to develop your skills and knowledge in areas in which you may have limited experience.

As an indicator of its effectiveness, a survey of practical test candidates (carried out by ORC International for DVSA) showed that, among those who had taken Pass Plus

- 93% felt more confident on the road
- 89% considered that their driving skills had improved.

This was as a result of taking the course.

> **Three ways to find out more**
>
> **1** Telephone **0115 936 6504**
>
> **2** Email **passplus@dvsa.gov.uk**
>
> **3** Visit **www.gov.uk**

* Subject to status. Candidates are advised to check available discounts with participating insurance companies.

What are the benefits?

Pass Plus will benefit you by

- enabling you to gain quality driving experience safely
- helping you to become a more skilful driver
- teaching you how to develop a positive driving style that's both enjoyable and safe
- reducing your risk of being involved in a road crash
- saving you money on your car insurance premiums.*

Pass Plus consists of a minimum of six hours' training, and the emphasis is on developing your practical driving skills. There's no test at the end. Instead, you'll be assessed throughout: you must cover all the modules to complete the training.

Enjoy the course!

Saving money on your car insurance should bring a smile to your face.

Developing your driving skills

Motorway driving

As a learner, you may have been able to experience motorway driving (see page 73). If you haven't, it's important that you understand the rules and regulations before you drive on your own on a motorway.

If you take Pass Plus, one of the modules relates solely to motorway driving. Alternatively, you can ask your instructor for motorway driving lessons. Either of these will give you valuable experience of motorway driving.

Further training

When you've successfully completed Pass Plus, you'll have demonstrated that you

- have developed your existing skills
- have acquired new skills and knowledge
- can drive safely in conditions not included in the driving test
- understand how you can reduce the risk of having a road traffic incident
- can maintain a courteous and considerate attitude to other road users.

Do you feel ready for the next level? If so, contact one of the organisations below.

DVSA has approved and monitors advanced driving tests offered by

 IAM RoadSmart
Tel 0300 303 1134
iamroadsmart.com

 DIAmond Advanced Motorists
Tel 020 8253 0120
advancedmotoring.co.uk

 RoSPA Advanced Drivers and Riders (RoADAR)
Tel 0121 248 2099
roadar.org.uk

section **five**
OTHER TESTS

This section covers
- o Towing a trailer
- o Retest for those who have lost their licence

Towing a trailer

You must have a full car* driving licence before you can tow any trailer or caravan. The key factor that determines what licence you need is the maximum authorised mass (MAM)** of the car and trailer.

If you passed your test before 1 January 1997, you can drive a car and trailer or caravan combination of up to 8.25 tonnes MAM.

If you passed your test after 1 January 1997, you can

- drive a vehicle of up to 3.5 tonnes (or 3,500 kg) MAM, towing a trailer of up to 750 kg MAM
- tow a trailer over 750 kg MAM as long as the combined weight of the trailer and towing vehicle is no more than 3,500 kg.

If you passed your test after 19 January 2013, you can tow

- small trailers weighing no more than 750 kg
- a trailer over 750 kg as long as the combined weight of the trailer and towing vehicle is no more than 3,500 kg MAM.

If you wish to drive larger car and trailer combinations, you'll normally have to take a further test (category B+E). Information about towing is available at **www.gov.uk**

Further information

Detailed information and advice about towing trailers can be found in *The Official DVSA Guide to Driving – the essential skills,* which can be purchased from good bookshops or by calling **0333 200 2401**.

Useful information on towing can also be found on the following websites

- **ntta.co.uk** (National Trailer and Towing Association Ltd)
- **caravanclub.co.uk**
- **campingandcaravanningclub.co.uk**

* A car includes any four-wheeled vehicle with a MAM of up to 3.5 tonnes that has no more than eight passenger seats.

** The MAM is the maximum permissible weight, also known as the gross vehicle weight.

If I don't fully load the trailer, can I tow a bigger one?

No, the size of trailer you can tow is dependent on the MAM, not the actual weight when loaded.

Do I have to take a theory test?

No, you've already passed a car theory test. There's no additional theory test for drivers towing trailers in category B+E.

Key towing skills

You should consistently drive to the level detailed on pages 20–71; that is, to at least **Level 5** in the *Driver's Record*, the standard required to pass a car test. There are, however, some differences and these are explained here.

Safety checks (page 26)

You need to know how to carry out checks on the condition of the trailer body, check that any doors are secure, and know how to load and secure a load to the trailer. At the beginning of the test, the examiner will ask you to explain or demonstrate five separate safety checks.

Mirrors (page 34)

You should know how to use additional mirrors and take relevant observation to compensate for the restricted view caused by large trailers and caravans.

Other traffic (page 42)

You should always show consideration for other road users by pulling up safely, when necessary, to allow others to pass and avoid the build-up of queues of traffic behind you.

Turning the vehicle around (page 52)

The 'turn in the road' exercise isn't relevant to towing, but you need to know how to turn so you can travel in the opposite direction; for example, using a roundabout or side roads.

Reversing (page 54)

There will be a different reversing exercise, which is normally carried out at the beginning of the test. You'll need to be able to reverse the car and trailer on a predetermined course to enter a restricted opening and then stop so that the extreme rear of the trailer is within a clearly defined area.

Parking (page 56)

During the test, you won't be asked to carry out a reverse parking exercise while on the road.

Emergency stop

There is no emergency-stop exercise for the B+E test.

Uncoupling and recoupling

You'll also need to be able to uncouple and recouple your car and trailer. This is normally carried out at the end of the test (see page 138).

Practising (B+E)

When you practise, you **MUST**

- display L plates to the front of the car and the rear of the trailer. These must be clearly visible. You may use D plates in Wales if you wish
- be accompanied by a person who's at least 21 years old and holds a full EC/EEA driving licence for category B+E (they must have held this for the past three years).

You should also practise reversing and uncoupling/recoupling your car and trailer. You'll be asked to do both these exercises as part of your test.

You should practise in all sorts of traffic conditions and on as many different roads as you can.

Your trailer **MUST** be laden for the test (see page 134), so you're advised to practice with a laden trailer.

Practise turning left and right, taking into consideration the extra length of the unit. Be aware of your trailer, especially when taking sharp turns.

Booking and taking your test

Book your test as you would a car test (see page 117). However, be sure to make it clear that you want to take a B+E test.

The test can only take place at test centres for drivers of lorries and buses, where there's a manoeuvring area. To find out where these are, ask your trainer, call **0300 200 1122** or visit **www.gov.uk**

Also, as the test is longer, there's a higher fee.

Documents

Make sure that you have your full licence with you and that it's signed. If your licence doesn't show your photograph, you must bring your passport. (Your passport doesn't have to be British.)

Only licences issued in Great Britain or Northern Ireland are acceptable. Your examiner can't conduct your test if you can't produce the correct documents.

If you don't have the correct documents or you forget to bring them with you, your test will be cancelled and you'll lose your fee.

Your test vehicle

The vehicle you intend to drive during your test should satisfy all the requirements given on pages 119–120 for those taking a car test. The L plates need to be displayed to the front of your car and the rear of your trailer. In addition, the vehicle should have an audible or visible warning device to confirm that the trailer indicator lights are operating.

The trailer being used for the test **MUST**

- have a closed box body
- be laden in accordance with the rules that can be found at **www.gov.uk**

Your test will be cancelled and you can lose your fee if your vehicle doesn't meet the rules.

Vehicle–trailer combinations should be fitted with nearside and offside externally mounted mirrors for use by the examiner,

and the car and trailer together must be capable of 62.5 mph (100 km/h).

Trailer loads must be either bagged aggregate or an intermediate bulk container (IBC) filled with water.

Your test

Your test will include the following parts:

Eyesight check Before you get into your car, your examiner will point out a vehicle at a suitable distance and ask you to read its number plate. You must satisfy them that you can read the number plate as detailed on page 10. If you need glasses or contact lenses to read the number plate, that's fine, but you must wear them during the test and whenever you drive.

If you can't speak English or have difficulty reading, you may copy down what you see.

If your answer is incorrect, your examiner will measure the exact distance and repeat the test. If you fail the eyesight test, your test will go no further.

Safety-check questions The examiner will ask you to explain or demonstrate five separate safety checks.

Extendable towing mirrors enable you to see what's behind you, rather than just seeing the side of the trailer or caravan.

The drive This will be approximately one hour long. It will include a wide variety of roads and traffic conditions, including roads carrying two-way traffic, dual carriageways and, where possible, one-way systems and motorways.

Your examiner will expect you to drive at least to **Level 5** standard and demonstrate all the key skills required in the car test. However, during the drive you won't be asked to

- do an emergency-stop exercise on the road
- reverse around a corner
- reverse park
- turn in the road.

Make sure that you negotiate all hazards and junctions safely by using good, all-round observation.

All practical driving tests include approximately 10 minutes of independent driving, during which you'll be asked to drive by following signs or a series of verbal directions, or a combination of both.

Reversing exercise This normally takes place before you leave the test centre but might be carried out at the end of the test. For full details of the reversing exercise, see pages 136–137.

Uncoupling and recoupling exercise For full details of the uncoupling and recoupling exercise, see pages 138–139.

The reversing exercise

The reversing exercise for this test will usually take place before you leave the test centre. You'll have to demonstrate that you can manoeuvre your car and trailer in a restricted space and stop at a specified point.

To carry out this part of the test, you should be able to reverse your car and trailer in a restricted space.

Your examiner will ask you to drive forward before you begin to reverse.

You should be able to do this inside a clearly defined area

- under control and in reasonable time
- with good observation
- with reasonable accuracy.

Your examiner will show you a diagram of the manoeuvring area and explain what's required. The size of the reversing area will be set out according to the size of your car and trailer together as a unit

- cone A1 is positioned 1 metre (just over 3 feet) into the area from the boundary line
- distance A to A1 is one-and-a-half times the width of the widest part of the unit
- A to B is twice the length of the car and trailer
- the overall length of the manoeuvring area will be four times the length of the car and trailer
- the width of the bay will be one-and-a-half times the widest part of the unit
- the length of the bay will be equal to the length of the car and trailer, up to a maximum of 12 metres. If the length of the car and trailer exceeds 12 metres, the bay will be set at 12 metres.

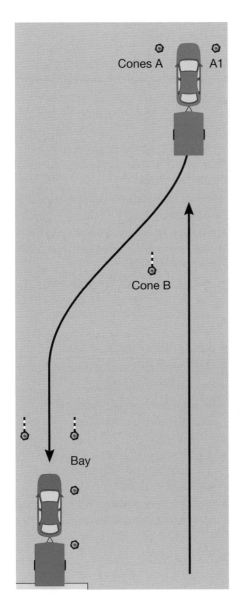

Tips from the experts

Approach cones A and A1 in a straight line and make sure that you stop at the cones; don't go too fast and go past them.

Turn the steering wheel the correct way as you start to reverse.

Keep in full control; don't let your wheel go over the yellow boundary or allow any part of your car to hit any of the cones or poles.

Use good all-round observation throughout the manoeuvre.

Make sure that you stop so that the rear of your car and trailer is within the yellow box.

What to expect on test

You'll be asked to

- drive forward and stop at a fixed point with the extreme front of your car level with, and in between, the cones A and A1
- reverse so that you pass cone B on the offside of your car
- stop so that the extreme rear of your trailer is within the painted yellow box at the end of the bay.

Uncoupling and recoupling

You'll need to be able to uncouple the car and trailer, park the car and then recouple the two safely. You need to gain the skills to do this safely before you drive with a trailer on your own.

When uncoupling, you first of all need to find a safe place with firm and level ground on which to carry out the procedure. Then you should

- ensure that the brakes are applied on both the car and the trailer (various parking mechanisms are fitted to trailers; you should consult the manufacturer's handbook to ensure that you operate yours safely)
- ensure that the jockey wheel, legs or other devices provided for supporting the trailer after uncoupling are lowered correctly. If there's any risk, strong planks or metal load spreaders should be used to distribute the weight
- disconnect the electrical line(s) and stow them away safely
- remove any fitted stabilising equipment
- remove any safety chain or coupling and move the car clear of the trailer.

When recoupling, you should treat the trailer as a new trailer that you haven't used before. You should

- ensure the brakes are correctly applied to the trailer
- move the car so that the trailer can be safely and easily coupled to it, and apply the parking brake
- attach the trailer to the car and check that the coupling is secure by using a method appropriate to the car and the trailer
- attach any safety chain or device
- fit any necessary stabilising equipment
- connect the electrical line(s)
- ensure that the wheels, legs or other supporting devices are raised and secured safely
- check the operation of the lights and indicators, and make sure the correct number plate is fitted
- release the trailer brake, ensuring that the car's parking brake is firmly applied.

What to expect on test

You'll normally be asked to uncouple
and recouple your car and trailer at the test
centre at the end of the test.

Your examiner will ask you to stop where
there's safe and level ground and then
uncouple your car from the trailer. You'll
then be asked to park the car alongside
the trailer before realigning the car with
the trailer and recoupling the two. Your
examiner will expect you to make sure
that the

- coupling is secure
- lights and indicators are operating
- trailer brake is released.

*When uncoupling or recoupling, make sure the
brake is correctly applied before you start.*

Tips from the experts

Make sure that you carry out the procedure
in the correct sequence, and that you can
do it confidently and without hesitating.

When uncoupling, make sure you've
applied the brakes to both the car and
trailer before you start and don't release the
trailer coupling without the wheels or legs
being lowered.

Don't try to move forward until the whole
uncoupling procedure has been completed.

When recoupling, make sure that the
brakes are applied on the trailer and that
you use good all-round observation as you
reverse.

Don't try to move away without raising
the wheels or legs and checking the
lights, indicators, safety chain and trailer
brake release.

Make sure that the jockey wheel is lowered
after uncoupling and then raised and
secured safely when recoupling.

Retest for those who have lost their licence

Losing your licence

If you lose your licence after being convicted of a driving offence, you may have to take a normal-length or extended driving test before you can recover your full licence.

The court can impose the following penalties

- an extended driving test for anyone convicted of a dangerous driving offence (this is an obligatory penalty)
- an extended driving test for anyone convicted of other offences involving obligatory disqualification
- a normal-length driving test for other endorsable offences.

If you've been given one of these penalties, you can apply for a provisional licence at the end of the disqualification period.

If your licence has been revoked under the New Drivers Act (see page 127), you'll also have to apply for a new provisional licence.

Provisional licence

The normal rules for provisional licence-holders apply

- you must be supervised by a person who's at least 21 years old and who has held a full driving licence for the category of vehicle being driven for the past three years
- the car must display L plates (or D plates in Wales) to the front and rear
- learner driver conditions apply to driving on the motorway (see page 73).

You'll have to pass the theory test before you can apply to take your practical driving test again. You should study the training materials before you take the test (see page 16).

Once you've passed the theory test, you can then apply to take your practical test.

Extended test

An extended test covers a wide variety of roads, usually including dual carriageways. This test is marked and assessed at the same level as a normal practical test, but it's more demanding because more time is devoted to normal driving. Make sure that you're ready.

Remember, the extended test lasts about 70 minutes. This is half an hour longer than the standard practical car test.

You're advised to take suitable instruction from an instructor.

You have to pay a higher fee for this test because of the longer duration.

What to expect on test In addition to the longer drive detailed above, your test will include all the exercises included in the normal test.

You'll be asked to carry out one of three possible reversing manoeuvres

- parallel park at the side of the road (see page 56)
- park in a bay (see pages 57–58)
- stop on the right-hand side of the road (see page 55).

You'll also be asked to carry out an emergency stop during the test.

There will be approximately 20 minutes of independent driving, during which you'll be asked to drive by following directions from a sat-nav provided and set by the examiner. One in five driving tests won't use a sat-nav; you'll need to follow traffic signs instead.

Your examiner will watch you and, in addition to the normal observations detailed throughout this book, will take account of your ability to concentrate for the duration of the test and your attitude to other road users.

annex
Private practice record

When you go out driving with a friend or relative, DVSA would encourage you to record the type of driving experience that you've gained.

You can use these forms to record what you did by ticking the appropriate boxes. You'll probably tick several for each drive; for example, it may have been light when you started to drive but dark by the time you finished. Take note of the time and mileage when you start, so that you can fill in how much time you spend on the road and how many miles you cover.

Fill in the time in hours (eg 0.5 hours) and the distance in miles (eg 20 miles). Visit **www.gov.uk** for further information and to download copies of these forms.

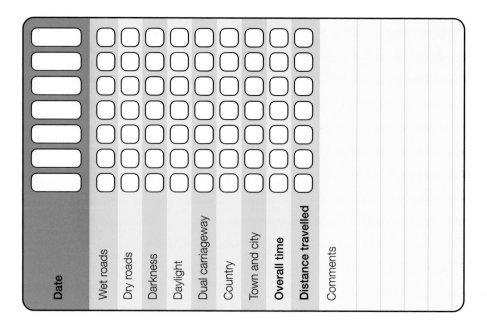

Date											
Wet roads											
Dry roads											
Darkness											
Daylight											
Dual carriageway											
Country											
Town and city											
Overall time											
Distance travelled											
Comments											

Learning to drive, ride or simply want to brush up on your knowledge?

- All the latest revision questions and answers
- Over 100 high-quality hazard perception clips
- Accessible on any internet-connected device

Visit **www.dvsalearningzone.co.uk** and enter code **SD10** to save 10%.

Revise on the go!

For everyone!

The Official DVSA Theory Test Kit for Car Drivers app

Give yourself the best chance of passing first time with the only Official DVSA Theory Test Kit app.

The Official DVSA Hazard Perception Practice iPhone app

The simple and convenient way to prepare for your hazard perception test on the go.

The Official DVSA Highway Code iPhone app

All the rules of the road at your fingertips.

SAVE 10% on official DVSA publications

Get ready to pass your theory and practical tests. Shop now at **www.safedrivingforlife.info/shop** and enter code **SD10** to **SAVE 10%** or call **01603 696979** quoting **SD10**.*

 safedrivinglife   @safedrivinglife   safedrivingforlifeinfo   safe.driving.for.life